Queens of Comedy

Studies in Humor and Gender

A series edited by Regina Barreca, *University of Connecticut, Storrs,* and Nancy Walker, *Vanderbilt University, Nashville, Tennessee*

Volume 1
Look Who's Laughing: Gender and Comedy
Edited by Gail Finney

Volume 2
Queens of Comedy: Lucille Ball, Phyllis Diller, Carol Burnett, Joan Rivers, and the New Generation of Funny Women
Susan Horowitz

This book is part of a series. The publisher will accept continuation orders which may be cancelled at any time and which provide for automatic billing and shipping of each title in the series upon publication. Please write for details.

Queens of Comedy

Lucille Ball, Phyllis Diller, Carol Burnett, Joan Rivers, and the New Generation of Funny Women

Susan Horowitz

Gordon and Breach Publishers

Australia   Canada   China   France   Germany   India   Japan
Malaysia   The Netherlands   Russia   Singapore   Switzerland
Thailand   United Kingdom

Amsteldijk 166
1st Floor
1079 LH Amsterdam
The Netherlands

British Library Cataloguing in Publication Data

Horowitz, Susan N.
  Queens of comedy : Lucille Ball, Phyllis Diller, Carol
  Burnett, Joan Rivers, and the new generation of funny
  women. - (Studies in humor and gender ; v. 2)
  1. Women comedians 2. Stand-up comedy 3. Comedy - Sex
  differences
  I. Title
  791'.0922

ISBN 2-88449-244-5

CONTENTS

CONTENTS

INTRODUCTION TO THE SERIES

Humor as a human activity crosses—and double-crosses—many lines and boundaries, including those of gender. *Studies in Humor and Gender* will explore these boundaries and the territories encompassed by them. The monographs and collections published in this series will provide useful and original perspectives on the interaction of gender and humor in many of their possible combinations. An interdisciplinary field by its very nature, the study of humor, comedy, joking, and play draws together the interests and expertise of those working in literature, anthropology, sociology, linguistics, communication, film studies, folklore, medicine, and, increasingly, gender studies. The works published under the aegis of *Studies in Humor and Gender* will offer scholars, writers, and general readers alike a forum for examining and discussing insights into a vital field of study.

By making available the best discoveries and theories about humor and comedy in books framed by issues of gender, we believe that this series will inevitably also shed light on the larger questions of culture, power, sexuality, and the imagination. Its texts will feature sound scholarship, integrative approaches to the study of humor and gender, and clear, lively prose. We have no doubt that the volumes published in *Studies in Humor and Gender* will generate interest, debate, dissent, recognition, and attention. Destined for personal bookshelves as well as libraries, these volumes will be widely read, consulted, quoted, and discussed both inside and outside classroom walls.

PREFACE

Why write a book about women and comedy? Isn't categorizing comedians by gender like classifying kisses by technique? The analysis diminishes the entertainment value.

Shouldn't we ask: is she funny? Not: is she feminine?

In fact, many comediennes describe comedy as "sexless." Some consider their chief mentors to be men. (Phyllis Diller was influenced by Bob Hope; Joan Rivers, by Lenny Bruce.) Some even describe comedy as "masculine"—this in spite of the fact that they are in the process of creating and performing it—sans penis.

A case can, and has been, made for considering comedy without reference to sex. Many books and articles have been written about comedy in general. However, I believe that exploring the art and lives of comediennes as women is valid. And more than valid. The art and lives of these gifted performers tell us a great deal about our own lives and the changing role of women in society.

A few facts:

1. Among many anthologies and studies of comedians, women are significantly missing or minimized. The norm is not neutral. It is male.

2. In the performing arts (music, dance, acting) the only profession where an overwhelming majority of performers are men is stand-up comedy. This partly, though not entirely, accounts for the focus of general anthologies and studies. The only show business profession where women significantly outnumber the men is stripping. (Some female jokesters combine comedy and stripping in routines like: "On my honeymoon, I wore a peekaboo blouse. My husband peeked and booed!" [Phyllis Diller] Or, as another comic remarked: "I know how to make men gay: I take my clothes off!")

However, despite barriers of macho tradition, women today form an exploding minority in the comedy field. Where they were once below 1% of stand-up comics, women are now 15–20% of the profession. And they are influential beyond their numbers. Unlike comedy clubs, which are male-dominated, situation comedies, with their vast entrée into tens of millions of homes, are female dominated (from *I Love Lucy* to *Mary Tyler Moore* to *Roseanne, Grace Under Fire* and *Ellen*). Most stand-up comics are eager to make the transition to the lucrative world of situation comedy. Stand-up comedy regularly provides television with performers. Many of these stars are women whose situation comedy characters are based on their own lives.

3. Most of us have noticed that in a mixed social situation, it is men who tell the jokes—particularly the raunchy ones. Women are

expected to laugh—though not the longest and hardest (especially at the raunchy ones), and not to top the men's jokes. One such activity I attended was termed (not-so-coincidentally) a "joke-off!"

On the other hand, most of us have witty female friends and family members. Funny women who have the talent and drive for performing careers achieve mass followings (and the fortunes that accompany their fame) by defying gender roles—doing physical, slapstick comedy (Lucille Ball), presenting themselves as homely tomboys (Carol Burnett), taking charge in comedy clubs (Phyllis Diller), or basing their act on intimate details of their own lives (Joan Rivers).

But no matter what success they achieve, comediennes have to deal with the conflict between a woman's prescribed role in society and her own personality, talent, and inclination. Female singers, dancers, and actresses pose few conflicts to their audience. Their talents enhance their attractiveness as women. Professionalizing their gifts might create the usual tensions between career and home life. But the simple expression of their talents doesn't make anyone call them unfeminine. Comedy does.

The growing presence of women in comedy shifts the definition of feminine from object (Henny Youngman's: "Take my wife, please!") to subject (Joy Behar's: "I want a man in my life, but not in my house. I want him to come in, fix the VCR, and leave!"). It's hard to keep women in their place as passive sex/domestic objects when they've just been actively using their life experience and opinions to get laughs.

Is there a contradiction between being feminine and being funny? Is there such a thing as a feminine style of humor? This book will explore these questions and others—such as the relation of the public personality of famous funny women to their private lives and to women's role in society.

For now, let me conclude by answering a very human question that I am often asked. When people find out that in the course of writing this book I interviewed Lucille Ball, Phyllis Diller, Carol Burnett, and Joan Rivers, they often ask: "What are they like in person?" And a funny thing comes to mind. Besides their obvious professionalism, they are still nurturing women. Maybe I looked skinny, or hungry, or whatever, but Lucille Ball pulled me in dripping wet from a rainstorm and gave me tea and cookies; Carol Burnett treated me to a substantial lunch; Phyllis Diller insisted on my taking home a huge fruit basket; and Joan Rivers made me scrambled eggs and toast.

In the course of researching and writing this book, I have become a fuller human being. And I hope that in the course of reading it, so will you.

ACKNOWLEDGMENTS

I would like to thank Lucille Ball, Phyllis Diller, Carol Burnett, Joan Rivers, Lily Tomlin, Joy Behar, Mo Gaffney, Rhonda "Passion" Hansome, Adrienne Tolsch, Lotus Weinstock, and a host of other comediennes who granted me extensive personal interviews. I would also like to thank my friends who offered their interest and support—especially noted theatre biographer Herbert G. Goldman for his thorough reading of my manuscript. I especially want to thank my parents, Isaac and Bess Horowitz, who gave me their unswerving encouragement and support. And finally, I want to thank all the wonderful performers and witty people who have made me laugh—or who have ever laughed at my jokes. Without you, none of this would have happened.

Without you, I couldn't share a laugh
Without you, I'd miss my other half
I'd feel so alone
I'd lose my funny bone
'Cause comedy's not something that you do all on your own
Without you, my spirits couldn't rise
My laughter is shining in your eyes
'Cause comedy takes two, it isn't something I could do
Without you.

Comic Appeal,
Sex Appeal, and
Power

The black and white television screen leaves the Jack-o-lantern orange hair to our imagination. But the pinned-up curls, saucer-sized eyes, silly putty mouth, and quavering "Ricky-y-y!" leave no doubt about who this is...and where we have tuned our television dial. Forty-plus years later, we still love Lucy.

Blue-gray smoke wafts past the two-drink-minimum cocktail glasses toward a wooden cigarette held by a skinny woman in a satin evening suit and frightwig. Her own explosive "Ah Ha-Ha-Ha!" jump-starts an echo of raucous laughter in the enormous nightclub. "Go Phyllis!" cheers a man in the audience—and Phyllis Diller punches home her next joke.

A Roman empress becomes a coughing co-ed, who turns into a Texas housewife, who metamorphoses into a wistful charlady, who sweeps up a fading spotlight as the final credits roll on the television screen. The hour-long variety show is over. The dozens of sketch characters have vanished—or been reborn in comic bits and pathetic shadings that color the full length roles created by...Carol Burnett.

"Can we *talk!?*" caws the thin, birdlike woman in the designer gown as her eagle eyes calibrate the carats on the engagement rings in the front row. Laughing hoarsely, Joan Rivers confides the latest dish—celebrity scandals, her most recent plastic surgery, or the secret of her success—real jewelry, fake orgasms.

1

Lucille Ball, Phyllis Diller, Carol Burnett, and Joan Rivers are Queens of Comedy. Each created a career that lasted over a quarter of a century. Each put her own twist on traditional female comic types and broke new ground for younger, more radical comediennes. And each is a very funny lady. For more than twenty-five years, these Queens of Comedy have been getting big laughs and big hands— winning hands, because they are in fact, top cards.

The Queen of Hearts is, of course, Lucille Ball. Her funniness and lovability charmed *I Love Lucy* fans in the 1950's and still appeals in today's syndicated re-runs. The situation comedy mixed broad farce with domestic sentimentality and fine, ensemble, comic acting. The emotional heart of the program was the love between Lucy and Ricky Ricardo (played by Desi Arnaz, Ball's husband, who produced the show). Like Ricky/Desi, millions of viewers said, "I love Lucy"— and crowned her the Queen of Hearts.

The Queen of Clubs is Phyllis Diller, who began performing in major comedy clubs and nightclubs at a time when stand-up comedy was 99% male. Diller broke down barriers against women in comedy through the sheer force of her talent and determination. At thirty-seven years old, Diller was a housewife with five children, an unemployed husband, and a gift for making women laugh at the laundromat. She embarked on a risky show business career where all the role models were male and seemingly inaccessible. She honed her talent until she developed herself into a grandmaster of comedy, writing much of her own material, playing clubs which seat thousands of people, and delivering twelve laughs per minute.

The Queen of Spades is Carol Burnett, who dug deeply into her own childhood pain (both parents were alcoholic and sporadically abusive) to create comedy that was darker and more violent than that of Lucille Ball. She broke new ground with her willingness to jump, trip, take pratfalls, mug, or do a Tarzan yell that challenged notions of ladylike behavior. Burnett has said:

> If you're a woman, it's difficult to break through the barrier of having others accept you as funny. There's all that training you've had since you were three. Be a lady! Don't yell or try to be funny. Just be a nice little girl. Sit quietly with your knees close together, and speak only when you're spoken to. Women are afraid to make themselves unattractive. I'm not afraid of that, goodness knows! But all but one in a million women are afraid to mess up their hair, not wear lipstick, slouch, look flat-chested....Most women are obsessed with an outmoded sense of modesty. They labor under the necessity of being ladylike. They are afraid that being funny is unfeminine.

Burnett's willingness to challenge that feminine role-stereotyping resulted in a style of comedy that mixed broad slapstick with vulnerability and pathos. Her talent and personal likability were at the core of *The Carol Burnett Show*, one of the few prime time television variety show to be hosted by a comedienne and the most successful.

Joan Rivers is the Queen of Diamonds. Her sparkling wit and hard-edged comedy cuts through pretense with the precision of an industrial strength diamond drill. Her love of jewelry is evident in her accessories: the necklaces, bracelets, brooches, and earrings that festoon her fashionable ensembles. Jewelry is also a favorite motif in her act, for show, for fun, and as a female success symbol, especially when set into engagement rings. For years, Rivers herself was a "diamond in the rough," polishing her act in low-pay, no pay showcase clubs. She broke taboos with her comedy act, basing it on her own life and daring treatment of intimate, female-oriented subject matter. She finally broke through on *The Tonight Show*, became Johnny Carson's first permanent guest host, and went on to host her own Emmy-winning talk show.

Each of these women had to struggle against some form of prejudice. Sometimes it was simple racism (Ball's sponsors resisted casting Desi Arnaz as her television husband because they did not think audiences would accept the idea of an American woman married to a Cuban). Sometimes it was internalized sexism—a fear of appearing unladylike or "not nice." For the first seven years of *The Carol Burnett Show*, Burnett was so concerned about being perceived as overly assertive and unfeminine, that she avoided attending production meetings where the show was planned and written.

Mostly it was unsubtle reminders that women, especially female performers, were meant to be pretty—that their success depended on their looks. Burnett and Rivers were discouraged from pursuing careers as actresses because they weren't "pretty" enough. Comedy provided an alternative to the "pretty" identity. Diller made her "ugliness" the cornerstone of her comedy act, and all three made fun of their appearance and lack of sex appeal.

As female stand-up comics, Diller and Rivers met with tremendous resistance. Stand-up comedy was—and to an extent, still is—a male profession. Many male comics got their start doing comedy in strip joints—and audiences were used to equating men with humor and women with stripping. As a beginning stand up comic, Rivers was booked into a strip joint and billed as "Pepper January—Comedy with Spice." When she kept her clothes on and tried to be funny, the frustrated audience booed her off the stage, yelling "Bring on the girls!"

Audiences at strip clubs have clear—if crude—expectations from female performers. They are different from general audiences in the graphic nature of their entertainment preferences. But are they different in kind? While there are male performers who are sex symbols, there is nowhere near the emphasis on attractiveness for male actors or even tv anchormen as there is for their female counterparts. Why are there so many more female strippers than male? Why are there so few women comics? Why is it that the *only* branch of show business where men significantly outnumber the women is stand-up comedy? And, conversely, why are today's female comics, while still few compared with the males, an exploding minority? (According to Budd Friedman, owner of the famous Improvisation Comedy Club in Los Angeles, about 15% of his comics are now women and their numbers are snowballing.)

Maybe it has something to do with how men look at women— and how women see themselves. For a long time, women were just not supposed to be funny. A 1909 newspaper editorialized:

> Measured by ordinary standards of humor, she is about as comical as a crutch....A woman was made to be loved and fondled. She was certainly not made to be laughed at.

This prevailing opinion led to the absurd situation of female humorists, who as Nancy Walker in her seminal book *A Very Serious Thing: Women's Humor and American Culture*, notes,"were writing humor in the face of the prevailing opinion that they were not capable of what they were at that moment, doing." Deanne Stillman, co-editor of *Titters*, a 1976 collection of women's humor, wanted to be a humorist since she was a teenager, but believing that "writing funny was something girls didn't do" signed the parodies she submitted to *Mad* Magazine as "Dean." In 1988, the owner of a well-known New York comedy club opined: "Stand-up comedy is aggressive. It takes balls. Sure some women do it, but you kind of wonder about them."

In 1996, Cary Hoffman, owner of Stand-Up New York comedy club, who admits he does not hire women as often as men, said, "Stand-up comedy has a lot to do with control and power. And most men seem to exercise it more easily than women."

Even some brilliantly successful female comics are infected with a vertigo that comes from trying to strike a balance between traditional sex roles and personal inclination. Joan Rivers has said, "I don't like funny women. I don't think I'm funny. I think I'm witty." Other female comics have simply faced the fact that they made a painful, but personally inevitable choice.

Gilda Radner said, "I know I've scared many men off because of humor. I'll be funny instead of feminine. You're not likely to see me sitting at the back of a party being pretty."

Karen Babbitt, a rising stand-up comic with big blue eyes and a mane of taffy-colored hair, comments:

> It's still not considered feminine to be really funny. To be successful, you have to sacrifice feminine approval for comedic approval. You have to come to a point where you don't care about getting feminine approval. My whole life I was miserable. I was always getting kicked out of class. I was not asked to the prom. I was not popular. I was infamous. It was extremely painful that I could not keep my mouth shut. Finally, when I became a comedienne, my life made sense. People say to me, "This must be the hardest thing in the world." For me, it's not. And it's not something I chose to do either. It's something that very specifically and methodically chose me.

Some comediennes have resolved the supposed conflict between funniness and femininity. Carol Burnett, stigmatized for years as a gawky "mugger," advised an audience at the Museum of Broadcasting that: "The idea that it's not feminine to clown around is old hat. Just be you." On a recent HBO special, stand-up comic Elaine Boosler dismissed the conflict with a breezy "being a lady has never been one of my goals."

What is the connection between comic appeal, sex appeal, and our notions of what is feminine? Why have so few women made it in stand-up comedy? And will this change as more "chick" comics rise up the pecking order of this cock-of-the walk profession?

It all does seem to have something to do with power—the power of comic appeal and sex appeal. The "life of the party" is usually the center of attention; and everybody laughs longest and loudest at the boss's jokes. The ability to be a good sport and laugh at a joke, especially when it's on you, is the mark of a good subordinate. Except in formally sanctioned "roasts" (which are often censored), no one expects the boss to have to "take it."

When you make someone laugh, you get him to accept the premise of your joke, which is often the stupidity of some officially sanctioned idea, behavior, or authority. Nancy Walker, author of *A Very Serious Thing: Women's Humor and American Culture*, comments:

> For women to adopt this role means that they must break out of the passive, subordinate position mandated for them by centuries of patriarchal tradition and take on the power accruing to those who reveal the shams, hypocrisies, and incongruities of the dominant culture. To

be a woman and a humorist is to confront and to subvert the very power that keeps women powerless, and at the same time to risk alienating those upon whom women are dependent for economic survival.

As for the motives of the jokester, at least some of them include a strong power drive. Professor Paul McGee, author of *Humor: Its Origin and Development*, asserts:

It seems clear that the need to dominate is one of the basic precursors for heightened humor development. The person in a small group or at a party who is the initiator of humor is really in control of the social situation; he gives people things that they respond to, so he's pulling the strings.

Psychologist Waleed Samaled adds:

The female stand-up comics have the same personality profile, aspirations, self-image, creative outlook, and ability as the men.

How do we feel about women pulling the strings—especially when they're attached to people's funny bones? The traditional matador/doormat format dictates that just as men are supposed to be taller, richer, smarter, and more aggressive, they are supposed to be the joke tellers, while the women laugh at their jokes. Ann Beatts, comedy writer, remembers what it was like to be an adolescent in the 1950's.

Real girls weren't funny. Real girls were pretty and fluffy and could do the splits in cheerleader tryouts. Real girls didn't crack jokes. Did you ever hear Sandra Dee crack a joke? Annette Funicello didn't even laugh; she just put her hands on her hips and got mad at Ricky or Tommy or Eddie or whoever was carrying her surfboard, so that they could tell her how cute she was when she was mad.

Unlike the male comic, whose talent and drive are supported by his sex role, the female comic often finds her inner nature at war with what's expected from "a real girl" or "a real woman." When Julia Klein interviewed several female comics for a 1984 *Ms.* article, she discovered:

The women agree that stand-up comedy is, in itself, an aggressive act; making someone laugh means exerting control, even power. But a woman cannot come off as overaggressive or she will lose the audience.

Comic Carol Siskind adds:

In a way, we have to be more careful. Men can be gross and get away with it. We have to be very careful not to step on the male ego. There are things you learn early on to phrase very carefully.

Things happen so fast in the comedy world, however, that Siskind's remark, made in the 1980's when she was was emcee at the defunct Improv on 44th Street, seems antiquated. Like feminism in general, women's comedy keeps pushing the envelope past old restrictions. Today's up-and-coming comics often do material that was once only heard on "party records" or "blue nightclubs." Even though Roseanne has softened her shtick for television audiences, her comedy has a coarse, caustically feminist edge that would have been unpalatable to audiences even a short time ago. Her nightclub act includes lines like:

I don't see why everybody says lesbians hate men. Why should lesbians hate men? They don't have to fuck 'em!

Even her scrubbed up television show features her chomping on a doughnut as she remarks:

A guy is a lump, like this doughnut. First you gotta get rid of all the stuff his *mom* did to him. (She whisks the nuts off the doughnut.) Then there's the macho crap they get from the beer commercials. And then, there's my personal favorite—the male ego. (She bites into the doughnut with savage joy.)

Unlike the slim, stylishly dressed, upwardly mobile, adorably madcap homemakers of 1950's sitcoms, Roseanne's TV alter-ego—a fat, disheveled, angry, blue-collar, working wife and mother demands that we pay attention to her unglamorized reality—and her opinions!

Nancy Walker says: "a common theme of women's humor is the desire to claim autonomy and power." In his article "Humor, Sex, and Power in American Society," Dr. Samuel Janus states:

Humor, effectively used, is a most potent source of power; it is especially needed and adopted by those who have no other recognizable form of power. Minority groups have long seized upon comedy as the expression of their will and power. The ability to make a person laugh with them, not at them, is a vital one.

Janus' insight most obviously applies to the Jews, a persecuted minority who have produced comedy writers, directors, and performers out of all proportion to their percentage in the population. The Jewish culture has historically idealized the intellect (including the ability to be funny) and denigrated violence. For Jews, humor has been a survival kit, a bittersweet elixir that transforms oy to joy. As Jews immigrated from European ghettos to Hester Street and even Hollywood, Yiddishkeit has flavored sitcoms, stand-up acts, and films and moved from the shtetl to the stars.

Of course, there are successful comediennes from all ethnic groups. Some of today's successful comediennes are African-American, like Whoopi Goldberg, Bertice Berrie, and Marsha Warfield; Italian-American like Joy Behar, Judy Tenuta, Fran Capo; Hispanic-American, like Marga Gomez; or Asian-American like Margaret Cho. If you're not an ethnic minority—it helps to feel like an outsider because of your looks, family background, disability, or personal history (Phyllis Diller, Carol Burnett, Geri Jewell, Rosie O'Donnell, or Brett Butler). Kate Clinton, lesbian comic, says:

> What's outside the norm is funny, so women are funny because the norm is clearly male. Lesbians are even further outside the norm than other women, so we're really funny.

Minority cultures are influenced by the mainstream and other subcultures. Jews learned to like hamburgers and Chinese food. Lenny Bruce blended American English with Yiddishisms and the improvisational stylings of Black jazz musicians. Women's comedy often mixes male comedy styles with female concerns. (Joan Rivers was most strongly influenced by Lenny Bruce; and Phyllis Diller's comic mentor was Bob Hope.)

It has always been more acceptable for masculine styles to influence feminine ones, rather than vice versa. Women wear slacks, man-tailored suits, shoulder pads, and even designer jockey shorts. Males in skirts, dresses, and feminine lingerie are more suspect. We accept it as natural that a subordinate group should copy the fashions of the dominant one. The powerless take on the trappings of the powerful, not vice versa. To most parents, a little girl who acts like a tomboy is cute; a little boy who acts like a sissy is embarrassing.

Like other groups that have suffered discrimination, women are classified as a minority by affirmative action programs. However, unlike ethnic minorities, women are a numerical majority and, rather than being segregated in ghettos, have been intimately involved with men. A woman's survival and comfort often depended on a man's willingness to care for her and her children. She needed to behave so that he would do so, in other words, be "feminine." What that often meant was mentally subordinate, dependent, and unchallenging. When a woman is funny, she presents herself as mentally strong and daring—challenging and mocking patriarchal assumptions. She risks alienating those upon she is dependent for survival.

In 1981, Janus wrote:

> The fact that women in comedy account for at most 12 percent of the field, whereas in other areas of show business they represent at least 50%, attests to their lack of credibility as power figures.

Lily Tomlin, commenting on why female comics sometimes encounter difficulties because of their gender, says:

> Funny is probably threatening, 'cause for people to laugh...it's submissive. When people laugh, they're vulnerable.

The feelings of release, the letting go that allows you to laugh, can be frightening to someone who feels that maintaining control is crucial to survival. Michael Iopoce, author of *A Funny Thing Happened on the Boardroom: Using Humor in Business Speaking,* says:

> Most pros agree that an all-male audience can often be the hardest to make laugh, while an all-female group is the easiest. And it has nothing to with a relative sense of humor. It's much less complicated than that. Humor successfully used, confers power or control over an audience. We must "let our guard down" to laugh. If we laugh too hard, we become "helpless" or "weak" with laughter. In our society, men are conditioned to avoid this at all costs. They are more reluctant to laugh than women, perhaps because they have been conditioned to avoid appearing weak, helpless, or just plain silly. Think about it—tough guys never laugh (except maybe when they're putting a few slugs into another tough guy). This sort of foolery becomes magnified when they are surrounded by other men. Who wants to be the first to let down his guard? It's just not macho.

Argus Hamilton, comic and m.c. at the famous Comedy Store in Los Angeles, prefers to think of himself as a "preacher" and the audience as his "congregation"—a benign model of domination. But he readily admits that many male comics describe themselves as "matadors" and the audience as a "lynch mob." If comedy is on some level a power struggle between comic and audience, what he-man wants to be beaten by a girl?

Iopoce offers advice to his reader on how to get around the problem of male resistance to humor.

> ...when facing an all-male audience, it's especially important to make sure you joke about something of common interest, so that you bond yourself with your audience—kind of become one of the guys, right? If

it's not a homogeneous group of men in the same company or the same field, the locker-room standbys are generally a good bet: sports, business, or—women.

Iapoce does not explain how a woman is supposed to become one of the guys (probably because his imaginary reader is male), especially if she has limited experience with team sports, business—or locker rooms. Presumably, she can joke about women (a subject about which she has considerable first-hand knowledge). However, her point of view may be different.

Kate Clinton does a sketch on the male-oriented porno film *Debbie Does Dallas*, where she muses on the cheerleaders in the shower room who keep washing their breasts. And washing. And washing their breasts—big circular motions.

> Well, we do know how dirty breasts do get. I, for example, sometimes change my bra three or four times a day.

And even if a woman makes herself the object of the joke, the very fact that she is taking center stage and making people laugh assumes authority.

> Passivity and wit are diametrically opposed; the former requires acquiescence to rules and the standards imposed by the dominant society, while the latter, with its associative values of intelligence, perception, and irreverence, implies the "tilting of unofficial values over official ones."

The notion that funniness implies power has a basis in the physiology of laughter. Basically, laughter is the build-up and sudden release of tension. Laughing means going along with a set-up, which builds intellectual or social tension and suddenly breaking the tension with an explosion of laughter, triggered by a punchline or comical action. The release is both intellectual (getting the joke) and physiological (laughter).

The person who laughs is rendered temporarily defenseless and physically weak—muscles relax, breathing becomes spasmodic, tears may come to one's eyes, and the laugher may even lose bladder control and fall down. (There is medical evidence that all this ultimately strengthens the heart, lungs, endorphins, and immune system, but that happens on an unconscious level. What the laugher immediately experiences is loss of control.)

Besides laughter, the body has other responses that involve increasing tension and sudden release, followed by deeper relaxation. They include yawning, sneezing, and…orgasm. Yawning and sneezing are passive responses to physical needs—sleep and irritation in the nasal passage. We don't seek them out or particularly enjoy them when they happen.

Laughter and orgasm are sources of pleasure. (Of course, there are fake laughs, usually done to placate someone in power or show that you get a joke (when, in fact, you might not enjoy or even understand it). A fake laugh is a lot like a fake orgasm—intended to smooth over a difficult social situation and not much fun for the laugher.)

Laughter and orgasm do seem to go together on an instinctive level—maybe that's why strippers and comics are often booked on the same bill. Strippers take off their clothes, and today's stand-up comics, who often base their comedy on their own lives, metaphorically bare their souls. Comedy and stripping are designed to give pleasure by stripping away respectable disguises. The audience responds with laughter or sexual arousal.

Both laughter and orgasm have intellectual and physical aspects. Of the two, comedy is more intellectual—getting the joke—resulting in a physical response—laughter. (Although physical tickling can produce laughter, it's not called comedy.) Sexual passion may involve very little conscious thought, and too much analysis, guilt, or worry can interfere.

Not much has been written about the relationship between laughter and orgasm, probably because of the difficulty doing research. (Imagine the classified ad—"Wanted: Sexual Surrogate with Great Sense of Humor.") But the fact is, you can't laugh and have an orgasm at the same time. The muscular tension that leads to orgasm dissolves in laughter. Comic Judy Carter, looking like Peter Pan in a lavender necktie, says:

> You can't be sexy and funny at the same time. Have you ever tried to have sex and laugh? It totally stops it.

The issue is complicated by the fact that funniness can be highly attractive. A good sense of humor is consistently listed as among the top ten qualities people seek in a mate. Desi Arnaz once noted that Ball was one of the few women who "could make you laugh, and yet at the same time, make you want to go to bed with her."

I suggest that while a good sense of humor can be appealing, when a relationship moves into the directly physical, the intellectual pleasure of comedy is distracting at best. And, if the humor is based on a kind of rapier wit, the effect may be chilling. An anonymous seventeenth century passage attributed to the comedic playwright Moliere says pointedly:

There is nothing more contrary to the passionate feeling of amorous pleasure than the intellectual pleasure which ridicule affords.

If laughter interferes with orgasm, sexual stimulation gets in the way of the mental focus necessary for comedy. Judy Carter says:

> Breasts aren't funny. If I have something tight on, they don't hear me. They look at me. It hits a different region. Comedy hits the mind—they laugh—it's an idea. But if you're hitting the groin.... (She tilts her head to the side in an idiot version of the RCA Victor dog.) Ever watch men in a strip club?

Perhaps this is why men who are threatened by female strength don't like funny women. Laughing means acknowledging their power. The slang of the stand-up comic succinctly sums up the power issues and the tension between humiliation and domination—either you "die" or you "kill." Either you "bomb" or you "murder the audience." Doing badly on stage can produce a state of fear physically manifest as "flop sweat." Doing well produces a state of exhilaration; the comic is likely to exult: "I slayed 'em!...I slaughtered 'em! I destroyed 'em!"

Sexual relations don't have to be experienced as humiliation or domination. Sexuality can be loving, mutual vulnerability—as can comedy. Lotus Weinstock, a comic who plays a sweetly spaced-out survivor of the sixties, says, "Comedy is a way of being the most intimate you can be with folks outside your home because when a whole roomful of people are laughing, suddenly you've dissolved the pain and shame of separateness. At that moment, there's no judgment—it's a true release."

Weinstock's opinion expresses an ease with vulnerability that many comics do not share. Eddie Murphy's humor is hard-edged macho: highly aggressive, frequently obscene, and anti-gay. Like his humor, his model for sex relations is a mutual power struggle, with women as "schemers" and men as "cheaters." As Murphy told a *New York Times* reporter: "The key to male supremacy is sexual performance.... After a woman has experienced a good orgasm, no matter what you do wrong, as long as you say, 'I'm sorry,' she will listen to your story."

The notion that male supremacy depends on sexual prowess is particularly strong in cultures where men are denied power based on income, profession, or education. Women's power was also traditionally limited, mainly to the bedroom and kitchen. The old model for the nuclear family was based on women supplying emotional nurturing to ambitious men—tending their personal needs, making a home, and raising the children. Not many men are willing to be house-husbands to ambitious women.

Today, however, the majority of women work outside the home. Even if both partners prefer that the wife be a full-time homemaker, most families need both incomes. Although most are in a pink-collar ghetto of low-paid service jobs, the percentage of women in the elite professions and management has risen dramatically since the 1950's. Women have moved from bedroom to boardroom and from house and garden to house and senate. And so, not so coincidentally, have funny women stepped out from standing behind Tom, Dick, and Harry, to standing behind the mike in comedy clubs.

And in fact, domestic fulfillment, even if fervently desired, is often fleeting. Divorce, a rarity in the early 1950's, has become commonplace. In the 1950's we had a cultural ideal of a nuclear family consisting of a breadwinner husband, housewife, and children. This was reflected in situation comedies like *Ozzie and Harriet, I Love Lucy, Leave it to Beaver,* and *Father Knows Best.* We now have a wide variety of family arrangements including single parents (Grace Under Fire) and an ever-increasing single, divorced, and widowed population—the "families" of *The Golden Girls, Designing Women, Friends, Cheers,* and *Seinfeld.* Most women on these programs work, whether in blue collar jobs *(Roseanne),* running a bookstore *(Ellen),* or managing a newsroom *(Murphy Brown).*

But, whenever there is rapid social change, there is conflict. The pressures that afflict other working women also impact on comediennes. The stress of life on the road—late hours, hanging around bars, and the general difficulty of establishing a supportive, steady relationship are especially hard on women. Male comics on the road are besieged by groupies. Not female comics. It's more comfortable for a man to hang around a strange bar than it is for most women. The social stress and loneliness may, to a large degree, account for the paucity of women comics.

Then too, women have traditionally been allowed less overt power than men; and a stand-up comic must control a crowd that is often hostile, rough, and drunk. Funny women have to achieve a delicate balance—projecting enough power to take control of the audience and enough vulnerability to be non-threatening.

Even comic actresses who don't have to directly confront an audience sometimes find their funniness makes them threatening. To appeal to audiences, comediennes (and/or the writers and directors who help create their characters) have sometimes made a trade-off, sacrificing either their sexuality or their intellect. They become "dumb blondes" or "wisecracking losers."

High-voltage sex appeal is compensated for by low wattage intellect. When a "dumb blonde" (or dizzy brunette) is funny (another form of power), she's not supposed to know what she's doing—she's only funny by accident. Like a child, she doesn't know she is amusing. "Dumb blondes" like Marilyn Monroe spoke in a whispery "baby voice" and masked their minds. Even when her character was not exaggeratedly sexy, holding a husband seemed to require sitcom stars like "dizzy brunette" Gracie Allen and "naive redhead" Lucy Ricardo to play dumb and be "unwittingly" funny.

As for the wisecrackers, they supposedly outsmart themselves when it comes to men. These ineffectual intellectuals may have brain power, but they are sexually neutered, as when the strip club audience screamed at Joan Rivers "Bring on the girls!" *Our Miss Brooks,* a popular 1950's situation comedy, starred Eve Arden as a wisecracking spinster schoolteacher who consistently failed to win the affections of her biology teacher heartthrob. The hit comedy *My Sister Eileen,* later musicalized as *Wonderful Town,* starred two sisters: a dumb one who was irresistibly pretty; and a smart one, who was a sexual loser. In a ruefully witty song, Ruth, the clever older sister, informs us that all she has been able to accomplish with her intellect is "One Hundred Easy Ways to Lose a Man." Like Miss Brooks and Ruth, Phyllis Diller and Joan Rivers, who were products of the same era, dazzle us with wit, while they portrayed themselves as sexual losers.

Self-deprecating humor is an issue for today's female comics. Many reject the old model of "dumb sexpot" vs. "smart spinster." Some look attractive and talk about husbands, boyfriends, and sexual pick-ups. If they are rejected or insulted, they respond with scathing, ribald wit. However, under the jokes, many of today's female comics have elements of the same "loser" persona that is at the core of the Diller/Rivers onstage character.

Has nothing changed? Are women performers still locked into old stereotypes about smart/funny vs. dumb/sexy? Yes and no. There are still comediennes who play out those roles. But there are many others who present themselves and their lives three-dimensionally. Yes, they are having trouble with relationships, but no, they are not passive victims. And if they don't look like cover girls—so what? Comedienne Maxine Lapidus speculates about the daily routine of ultra-thin models:

What do these women do all day? They wake up in the morning. Eat a blueberry. "Oooh! I'm full!" They go back to sleep.

Mimicking the projecting bust/buttocks posture and half-closed eyes/half-open mouth of a *Cosmopolitan* cover girl, Sandra Shamus notes ironically, "This is a *natural* pose for women," and adds ironically, "I have never heard anyone say anything intelligent in this position."

Joy Behar speculates that women's problems stem from being born at the wrong time:

> This is the wrong century to be a woman. The best time to have been a woman was when Rubens was a painter, the fat century. In that period, if you weighed 300 pounds, you could be a model. Christie Brinkley would have been a hat check girl. Roseanne—Miss Milan, 1537. In that century, you could really have an attitude: "What d'ya mean, no dessert? I've got a sitting with Caravaggio. If that man doesn't see some cellulite, I'm history. Now hand me that cannoli, you piece of...."

If, today's comediennes have trouble getting a guy—they impute the problem not to their own lack of appeal but to the men's lack of ability to communicate, or commit—or simply to the fact that in the marriage market, even inferior men have a statistical advantage over women. Instead of longing for someone rich and handsome, it's "any mammal with a day job."

Sex appeal has always been in the eye (or ear, or touch, or brain) of the beholder. And types of female beauty go in and out of fashion. What another age called Rubenesque, our own calls overweight. Is a high fashion model a sophisticated sylph? To a culture that links plump curves with femininity, fertility, and food, she is merely skinny. Hard bodies were not appealing when women of leisure were expected to be passive, physically weak, and inactive. In the case of comediennes, the charm of off-beat attractiveness outshines conventionally perfect features.

Does this mean that we have moved beyond rigid sex roles? Are today's female comics free to be as funny, smart, attractive, and unrestrained? Contemporary women comics are much more apt to publicly use the kind of language that was formerly restricted to all male bars and locker rooms. We have always had "dirty" women comics like Belle Barth and "Moms" Mabley. But they tended to perform in special nightclubs that catered to blue humor, and they usually presented themselves as old and unattractive—their lack of personal sex appeal giving them a license for bawdiness. What is new in mainstream clubs is the use of "dirty" material by attractive, young women. (Not that all women comics—or all male comics—work "dirty." The chance to go on television—where the big money is—as well as personal inclinations dictate that many comics work "clean.")

Many people find "dirty" female comics offensive. If so, we should keep in mind that they are are echoing a style that works in many comedy clubs—where most of the comics are men. Many of today's female stand-up comics adopt the aggressive, crude posture popularized by male comics, not only to express their own anger, but also in order to establish their right to stage turf with rowdy crowds.

But unlike male comics, who are often besieged by groupies, female comics often find that their onstage aggression is viewed as an offstage threat. Or else they find themselves judged by a double standard. Comic Karen Babbitt says, "Male comics can do stuff with heavy sexual overtones, which women cannot successfully do. And they can be more aggressive in handling hecklers. A male comic can say, 'I can piss on you from here,' and get a big laugh."

Then too, by nature or training, most female comics (like most women) tend to be less aggressive than their male counterparts. Lenny Bruce aggressively used comedy to challenge social taboos and broke down many barriers of what was permissible in stand-up comedy. Bruce exerted a strong influence on both male and female comics, for example, Joan Rivers. Rivers broke many taboos for mainstream female humor, but she never went as far as Bruce. And there is no woman doing the hostile, scatological humor of Andrew Dice Clay.

Lotus Weinstock adds:

> Just as women have a problem being dynamic or bawdy or loud or intense on stage, the men have a problem showing their vulnerability. The better male comics are now showing weakness in a way that's acceptable for men. But there's just so far the audience will allow you to go.

Wherever women comics are going, it seems to be on the cutting edge of what is permissible for women in general. Although social wit has always been an attractive feminine attribute, aggressive or crude wisecracks have been problematical, Shared laughter breaks social tension, allows people to relax, creates a bond, and gives pleasure. But women have been expected to temper their own natural humor in the name of ladylike femininity—on stage and off. Helene Johnson, Chief Executive Officer of CALTOY says:

A woman can laugh at the jokes, and show that she understands the dirty words, but she shouldn't laugh the longest or the loudest. And she shouldn't try to top the men's jokes. She'll get the laugh, but she'll be considered a "broad."

Corporate life depends on smooth social relations and respect for hierarchy. Social manners tend to be conservative. Stand-up comedy often provides audiences with relief from hierarchy and the repressive rules of the workplace and polite social life. Comics are encouraged to be daring—either mildly titillating or downright shocking. The gifted comic shoots a sandblast of truth that clears the dust off a facade of social manners. But ladies have been expected to uphold traditional morals and manners. Female comics are expected to go farther than civilian funny women—but not too far.

If the sexual frankness of some of today's popular female comics partly reflects the styles of their even bawdier male comics, is there a counter-influence? Do female comic styles impact on male comics? Are we moving toward a more androgynous style of comedy? There are superficial signs of androgyny in other fields and aspects of social life. Since the 1960's, long hair on males has been a badge of youthful rebellion. It's less popular now among the general population, but it endures among male rock musicians. Businessmen in creative fields sometimes sport little pony tails; and hip, heterosexual males sometimes wear earrings.

Will a more feminine style of comedy become "hip"—for both male and female comics? Today, there are both numerically more comediennes whose comedy expands beyond traditional "female" areas. Will they influence more men to move toward a less macho and more humanistic styles? Jay Leno, comic and host of *The Tonight Show* comes out of the 60's generation—a generation whose consciousness was profoundly influenced by the sexual revolution and women's and men's liberation movements. He has seen his own stand-up comedy field change from an almost exclusively male domain to a profession that includes more and more women. Not so coincidentally, his comedy is politically aware, humanistic, and sometimes feminist. Reviewing the movie *Big*, where a pre-pubescent was trapped in Tom Hanks' body, he commented:

A grown man acting like a twelve year old? Now there's a shock!

What is the road of the future? Will comediennes follow in the footsteps of macho comedy styles, salting their vocabulary with profanity and donning aggressive posturing like shoulder pads and pinstripes? Will the mood of the country—and the comics—become more conservative—dividing men and women into traditional sex roles? Or will both women and men comics move toward a comedy style based less on a power model of domination and submission and more on sharing?

All artists mirror their society. This is especially true for comics, whose art is validated not by its impact on a small group of connoisseurs or succeeding generations, but on the instant feedback of laughter. Comics who comment on contemporary mores exert an influence on their fans that is more powerful than that of standard, and duller authority figures.

The growing numbers of women comics reflect changes in sex roles and challenge our traditional notions about men and women. Lucille Ball, Phyllis Diller, Carol Burnett, Joan Rivers, and all other comediennes past and present, are rooted in a tradition of female comic personae. The seed of their individual talent is nurtured—or twisted—by the needs and beliefs of their contemporaries. The more adventurous among them break new ground, challenge their audience, and open up possibilities for a new generation of performers. By studying the art of popular comediennes, we may learn what it means to be female and professionally funny—and something about what it means for a woman to exert power.

We must all deal with issues of sex-roles and power. It is the special task of the comic to handle these issues with charm and humor. By looking into their "funny mirror," we may learn something about our own ambivalence about comic appeal, sex appeal, and power. We may learn something about masculinity and femininity. And we may learn something about ourselves.

Sources

Barr, Roseanne, *I Enjoy Being a Girl*, Hollywood Records, 1990.

Barreca, Regina, Editor, *Last Laughs,* (New York: Gordon & Breach, 1988), p.145.

Burnett, Carol, as quoted in *Women in Comedy,* Linda Martin & Kerry Segrave, (Secaucus, New Jersey: Citadel Press 1986), p.330.,

Horowitz, Joy, "June Cleaver Without Pearls," *The New York Times,* October 16, 1988.

Horowitz, Simi, "Comedy Tonight!" *Backstage,* April 19, 1996.

Horowitz, Susan, "Women Comics Come On Strong" *Los Angeles Herald Examiner,* September 10, 1981.

Iopoce, Michael, *A Funny Thing Happened on the Way to the Boardroom,* (New York: John Wiley & Sons:1988). p.20.

Janus, Samuel S., "The Comic Personality," *The American Journal of Psychoanalysis*, 1981, p.52.

Janus, Samuel S., "Humor, Sex, and Power in American Society," *The American Journal of Psychoanalysis*, Summer, 1981.

Johnson, Helene, personal interview, conducted in 1990.

Lauter, Paul, *Theories of Comedy*, Anonymous (Moliere?) from "Letter on the Impostor *(Tartuffe)*." p.150.

Leno, Jay, *The Tonight Show*, NBC, 1988.

Martin, Linda and Segrave, Kerry, *Women in Comedy*, (Secaucus, NJ: Citadel Press) pp.385, 368.

McGhee, Paul, *Humor: Its Origin and Development*, 1981, as quoted in *Psychology Today*, p. 27.

Rivers, Joan, personal interview conducted in her home in Bel Aire, California, 1980.

Samaled, Waleed as quoted in *Psychology Today*, p. 28.

Walker, Nancy, *A Very Serious Thing*, (Minneapolis:University of Minnesota Press, 1988), pp.9, 79, 26.

Warren, Roz, Editor, *Revolutionary Laughter*, (Freedom, CA: 1995)

Wisecracks: a documentary film directed by Gail Singer, Produced by Gail Singer and Signe Johansson in co-production with Zinger Films and The National Film Board of Canada, Distributed by Alliance International, 23 Prince Andrew Place, Toronto, Canada M3C 2H2. © 1991, (Publicity: Lauren Hyman, 799 Greenwich St., New York, NY 10014).

Lucille Ball

The baby-blue, mascara-spiked eyes widen, the head tilts, the electric orange curls bob, and the wide, lipsticked mouth takes another sip of "Vitameatavegamin syrup." *I Love Lucy* is back on the air for its latest re-run. Eager to do the commercial that will launch her in show business, Lucy Ricardo downs the nutritional syrup, unaware that the concoction contains twenty-four percent alcohol. As she extols the virtues of the product, her eyelashes bat their way past an inner fog, and her face slips into silly putty stupefaction. Innocent, child-like Lucy, is thoroughly drunk—and very funny.

Unlike Lucy Ricardo, her famous situation comedy alter-ego, Lucille Ball was not particularly naive. By the time *I Love Lucy* went on the air in 1951, Ball was over forty and had been in show business, playing mostly glamour roles, for twenty years. She was born in Jamestown, New York on August 6, 1911. Her mother was a concert pianist, and her father, who died when she was four, was a mining engineer. At the age of 15, Lucille went to New York, where she enrolled in the John Murray Anderson Dramatic School. She obtained chorus jobs with various Broadway productions, but the shows never went beyond the rehearsal stage. Because of the touring companies she had seen as a child in Jamestown, she originally wanted to be in vaudeville. But by the time she arrived in New York City, the era of the great vaudeville stars was over. Or, as Ball notes, "Vaudeville was dead, but I didn't know it!"

To pay the rent, she worked as a model and showgirl. Despite her statuesque figure, the work did not come easily to her.

> I wasn't trained, I couldn't sing, dance, or perform in any way. I was as untalented as they come. I couldn't even walk correctly. I was very shy—terrified of the girls around me and the people in the audience. I'd walk stiffly across the stage, and they'd say, "Couldn't you walk more like a showgirl? You are a showgirl, you know." I had to learn everything.

Broke, and surviving on a diet of coffee and the doughnuts she could steal off lunch counters, Ball collapsed of rheumatoid arthritis. She went home and rested for three years. When she recovered, she returned to New York, where she ran into a friend who knew an agent who needed showgirls for *Roman Scandals*, an Eddie Cantor picture. Producers were in the habit of doing line inspection of the showgirls. Ball, who wasn't quite as stacked as some of the others, stuffed her bodice with toilet paper—some of which was trailing out when the producer came by. Lucille Ball comments dryly:

> I may not have been as beautiful as some of the other showgirls, but he certainly noticed me. And I was in show biz! Everything on that set was interesting! I was learning how to act with the people—to become a part of the whole studio. There were spots where they needed a girl to scream or get chased by alligators. Some of the other girls were asked and they said, "Why? That's a nothing bit!" But I was tickled to death. It gave me a chance to work with Eddie Cantor and to work longer on a scene. The director would say, "You need somebody to do what? Why don't we get that girl who ran through with the duck?" They knew I'd run, I'd scream, I'd fall—I'd do what I was asked to do. I never complained. I didn't care that they didn't even know my name because nobody knew who I was anyway. That's the way I thought from the beginning, which was a big help.

Ball went on to play in *Room Service* with the Marx Brothers. She also appeared with The Three Stooges, Laurel and Hardy, and most major male comics. But she was more impressed with glamorous female stars.

> I was interested in certain actresses' looks. I admired the way Rosalind Russell could be the career woman and look uppity and deliver the lines so sharply. I admired Carole Lombard from the word go—every suit she wore, every time I saw her hair—I loved her. And she was a good friend of mine. But I didn't model myself around anyone. There wasn't that kind of personage around me—except Carole Lombard, and

she was doing sophisticated comedy—so was everyone else. They weren't doing the crazy kind of domestic comedy that we did eventually.

Ball herself, was mainly considered for dramatic, glamourous parts: hard-bitten models and showgirls.

I had to start as a model because I looked like a model. And I had to start also as "the other woman" or "career girl" because I had a lousy voice. I have a deep, guttural voice that has no softness or romanticism. It's aggressive. I've always had it, no matter how I try to dolly it up.

Ball scored some of her biggest successes in "tough girl" roles. In the Dorothy Arzner film *Dance Girl Dance,* she played a burlesque dancer; and in *The Big Street,* she played a vixenish nightclub singer who is crippled by a gangster. She was also occasionally cast as an ingenue—her role in *Too Many Girls,* the picture that brought Desi Arnaz out to Hollywood and occasioned their meeting.

According to his autobiography, when Arnaz first saw her, she was still in costume from another movie and "She looked like a two-dollar whore who had been beaten by her pimp, with hair all over her face and a black eye." When he saw her later, out of costume, wearing slacks and a sweater, Arnaz found her more attractive, and she responded to his ploy to teach her to rumba. "He had a snazzy line," says Ball tartly. "But we never did get around to dancing." After each had shed a then current lover, they moved in together, married, and began the sequence of events (including one never-consummated divorce in 1944) that led to *I Love Lucy.*

Meanwhile, Ball's image was gradually taking form. She was becoming someone recognizable and likeable—a personality "type."

When I was starting out, I made five, six pictures a year. I never knew what happened to them—sometimes I never even got invited to the preview. I played all kinds of small parts—no characters that anyone would recognize or care about. Then I got bigger parts. Finally, the biggest thrill I ever got—I'd been at RKO about four years and Mr. Piatzig called me into the office. He showed me the first three pages, and it said, "Lucille Ball type." It wasn't exactly what I did in Lucy, but it was a zany, domestic comedy, and it helped me years later. With the advent of television, besides being typed, you were in someone's living room every week.

By 1947 Lucille Ball was appearing in a radio show called *My Favorite Husband,* which was sponsored by CBS . Ball's co-star was Richard Denning; and she played Liz, a madcap wife married to Denning's George, a staid, midwestern banker. This early training in radio taught her to time the reading of her lines to laughs coming from the live audience. Later on, for much the same reason, *I Love Lucy* was filmed in front of a live audience. She also began to lay the foundations for comedic timing as the byproduct of ensemble acting. Even in the early days as a nameless Goldwyn Girl on the studio lot, she had wanted to learn to act and react—to respond to what other performers were doing. Radio, with its emphasis on listening, helped her to translate her response into aural terms.

> You cannot teach timing. But as close as I've come to it—is to listen. Now you're in a scene, and you are speaking, and I ostensibly will have the topper to the scene. My procedure is: you are speaking, I am listening. Then I react to what you've just said, and then, I act—I give you my line. In that process has been a timing. If I took the time to listen, react, and then act, the timing was there by itself. But if I had been sitting there, and I'm thinking about my last line and my topper, and I didn't listen or react—there went the timing. The first thing is to listen.

In 1950 CBS informed Donald W. Sharpe, the Ball/Arnaz manager, that they wanted to transfer Lucy's radio show *My Favorite Husband* to television. Jell-O was willing to continue its sponsorship, but only if Ball and Denning were retained as the leads. When Ball requested that Arnaz play her husband in the television version, the television officials refused. "We don't think viewers will accept Desi, a Latin with a thick Cuban accent, as the husband of a typical, red-headed American girl like Lucille Ball. Of course, we adore Lucy and want her to be in the show."

Mrs. Arnaz, then thirty-eight, stood firm: no Desi, no show. This unusual display of marital devotion may have been prompted by her sense that her ten-year marriage, propped up by a Catholic wedding ceremony on June 19, 1949, was falling apart. While Ball was doing the radio show and fulfilling some film commitments, Arnaz was traveling around the country with his rumba band. Their sexual jealousy, fueled by Desi's reputation as a womanizer, led to long distance quarreling. Working together offered a chance to ease the tensions of frequent separations.

However, attempting their own television series entailed financial risk. By now, Lucille was doing moderately well with her motion picture and radio career, and Desi was netting over $100,000 a year as a bandleader. Not only was the medium of television relatively untested, CBS executives insisted that a Ball/Arnaz combination would flop with audiences.

To prove their appeal as a performing couple, Ball and Arnaz decided to create a vaudeville act. They formed Desilu Productions, named after their California ranchette. To coach them, Arnaz called on Pepito, the Spanish clown, who had headlined at the Hippodrome and had done command performances for European royalty. Pepito concocted some bits for Ball and Arnaz and coached them in the skits. Arnaz rented a suite, and for two weeks they rehearsed.

In the act, Lucy, in baggy pants and a frightwig, played an inept musician who is desperate to get into show business. Arnaz played bandleader/straightman, and they set out on a twelve-week vaudeville tour. Their routines called for Ball to act like a seal, burping out notes on horns and waddling on her tummy across the stage. She also made use of a outsized prop cello, out of which she pulled a stool, a horn, a toilet plunger, gloves, flowers, and a violin bow. These vaudeville bits were so successful that they became highlights not only of the tour, but later of the pilot film for *I Love Lucy*. Ball credits her finesse in handling props to Buster Keaton, with whom she once shared an office at MGM.

> I went on tour with my entire act in a cello case. He taught me never to let it out of my sight. Never to leave the train without it. Never to depend on its being there at the theatre. Never entrust it to a stagehand or anyone else, and rehearse with it every day.

Madelyn Pugh and Bob Carroll, Jr., who were writing Ball's radio show with Jess Oppenheimer, also wrote a short sketch for the act. The writing team was to last through 180 half hours of *I Love Lucy*, plus twelve hours of *The Lucy/Desi Comedy Hour*, a number of *The Lucy Show* episodes, and many of the *Here's Lucy* shows. Ball gives full credit to her writers for the visual, slapstick comedy that became her trademark.

> It's all right there in the script. We had started out together in radio, and at first they didn't know what I could do physically, because in radio you stand and read. Later on, when we got to television, they were writing block comedy scenes for Vivian and me, and somebody said, "That's just like a Laurel and Hardy scene." And I said, "Yeaeaeaeah...!" That was after two years of working in television. I didn't even know that we were doing Laurel and Hardy.

During their New York booking, Lucille became pregnant. The Arnazes canceled the last half of their tour and modified Ball's onstage acrobatics, cutting out the bit where she wiggled on her stomach. The couple returned to California, but within two days Ball was rushed to the hospital where she suffered a miscarriage—her second. It was a traumatic experience for the couple, who had tried for over ten years to have a child. Ball flung herself into her work, finishing her commitment to *My Favorite Husband* while begging her manager to find a television show to do with Arnaz. Then, in October, three months after the miscarriage, Ball again found herself pregnant.

By December their agent had negotiated a deal with west coast CBS for a pilot film. However, William Paley, who ran the network from its corporate headquarters in New York, overrode the decision and agreed only to sell Desilu air time—if Ball and Arnaz would finance the pilot. Many advised the couple that they were committing career suicide by risking film, radio, and band commitments to take a chance on the untried medium of television. Ball remembers:

> It was then that I dreamed about Carole Lombard. She was wearing a very smart suit, and she said, "Go on, honey. Give it a whirl!"

The network assumed that the Arnaz's would be moving to New York to start the show. Since most television watchers were on the East Coast, the sponsors wanted the show to broadcast live from New York, while the rest of the country would see it rebroadcast in lower quality kinescope (filmed from the television screen). Since Ball was by now very pregnant, the Arnaz's wanted to remain at home in California.

Arnaz suggested that *I Love Lucy* be shot in California on 35mm film, which produced a better quality print than kinescope—what everyone beyond the range of live transmission saw when they watched television. Film, however, had two drawbacks: higher production costs and the problem of using a live audience on a film set.

CBS and Philip Morris finally agreed to contribute an extra two thousand dollars apiece—if Ball and Arnaz would take a salary cut. Arnaz agreed—asking for 100% ownership of the show in return—and the network agreed. This decision, which set a model for the shooting of television programs, accounts for the availability of broadcast quality Lucy shows that are still seen daily by over two million viewers. It also made Ball and Arnaz multi-millionaires.

The technical problems of filming a situation comedy complete with live audience were challenging. For this, Arnaz tracked down Karl Freund, the legendary German cinematographer. Freund had developed the exposure meter, first exploited the moving camera (utilizing dollies and cranes), and was credited with inventing the "process shot"—shooting live actors (often in a moving vehicle) in front of a transparent screen on which a background is projected.

The design for the show called for minimal sets—central living room with kitchen at right and bedroom on the left and uniform lighting. The show was filmed with three cameras in front of a live audience. This method, attributed to Desi Arnaz, resulted in a filmed/edited product which could be corrected in post-production and enhanced with a laugh track, as well as opticals such as wipes, fades, and dissolves. Unlike the low-resolution kinescope, the "Lucy" show was a tangible product with a long life which could be effectively marketed long after the live broadcast. (In fact, more than forty years later, it still generates revenue in syndication.)

After sacrificing salaries for ownership, Ball and Arnaz were able to reap a windfall from I Love Lucy and fund "Desilu" (named after the couple's ranch—his name first) headed by Arnaz. A shrewd and innovative businessman, Arnaz's on screen presence as Ricky Ricardo, romantic Latin crooner, belied his real entrepreneurial talent and toughness (much as Lucy Ricardo's laughably inept housewife belied Lucille Ball's comedic genius, perfectionism, and ambition). Desilu went on to make hundreds of hours of programming, using essentially the same method. Investing the profits from I Love Lucy, Arnaz produced December Bride, Make Room for Daddy, The Ray Bolger Show and The Untouchables, and built Desilu into a vast studio empire. Desilu eventually purchased RKO, Ball's former studio. With thirty-five movie stages, a forty acre backlot, and offices along with the Motion Picture Center, Desilu grew bigger than MGM or Fox.

The three-camera set up, central living room (or workplace), studio audience, frontal staging, and laugh track have (with minor variations) endured for over forty years as a time-tested formula for situation comedy. The home setting,which was Lucy's workplace, and the nuclear family have expanded to include outside workplaces like newsrooms (Mary Tyler Moore, Murphy Brown) "families" of co-workers, single parents (Grace Under Fire) and friends (Golden Girls, Ellen, Seinfeld, Friends), but the basic format of situation comedy has endured as the most consistent generator of income and audiences for television.

A key factor in I Love Lucy's appeal is its roots in even older art forms—vaudeville, radio, and film. Ball may have quipped that "vaudeville was dead" by the time she arrived in New York to begin her career. But ironically, it was the success of Ball/Arnaz's touring vaudeville act that persuaded CBS executives to offer Desilu air time. The original pilot for the television show, based on the vaudeville act, featured lots of broad slapstick, props, and Desi's band, all woven loosely together around the premise that Lucy wants to get into show business.

The couple grafted Ball's slapstick and Arnaz's music onto a domestic comedy format. The domestic situation comedy was well-established on the radio (Ball's own show *My Favorite Husband* pre-saged Lucy). What propelled Lucy into the stratosphere of superhits was Ball's genius for visual mimicry and physical comedy—irrelevant on the radio, but crucial in film. (Silent film comedy was heavily influenced by vaudeville.) Desilu's writers Pugh, Carroll, and Oppenheimer, freely admitted mining films for bits and story lines. Lucy not only borrowed from Keaton, Chaplin, Harpo Marx, and Laurel and Hardy, she imitated Katherine Hepburn, Tallulah Bankhead, Marilyn Monroe, and Anna Magnani. (Lucy's hysterically funny grape-squashing sequence is a take-off of 1950's Italian neo-realism.)

The domestic appeal of the series depended on extracting its entertainment elements from their show business roots (the world of Ball and Arnaz) and melding them into middle class life—the world of their viewers. When writers started submitting scripts for a series, they based the lead characters on Ball and Arnaz, portraying them as Hollywood types. Ball disagreed.

> After I'd read one or two, I said "No way! These people must not live in Hollywood. Everyone in the world thinks that everybody in Hollywood has two cars, a swimming pool, and no problems. We have to have economic problems. It has to be identifiable with middle America. If the washing machine breaks—it's a disaster. If I want a new dress, I have to scheme for it."

The decision to place *I Love Lucy* in a drab apartment gave the show its "common touch." Like *The Honeymooners, All in the Family,* Carol Burnett's *Eunice* episodes, *Roseanne,* and *Grace Under Fire,* the comic antics of the characters are grounded in everyday reality. Since Lucy's schemes often tended toward the absurd and implausible, anchoring them in mundane, domestic life provided the show with audience identification. Instead of playing a Hollywood actress like herself, Ball played an ordinary housewife whose dream of getting into show business is every housewife's dream of a more glamourous, adventurous life.

> Housewives all over the world could identify with those situations, and they would love to have carried them as far as I did and have as much fun with them. It was an exaggeration of things that happen in every household, especially where there's an economical cut-off,

where you don't have money for everything and you've got to scheme to make ends meet.

Along with the setting, the name of the series also underwent some evolution. CBS did not want to give Arnaz star billing at all and proposed calling the show "The Lucille Ball Show" and, in smaller letters "co-starring Desi Arnaz." When Ball objected, the network offered "The Lucille Ball and Desi Arnaz Show." But she again refused—her name came first. Finally, someone from the Biow Agency suggested "I Love Lucy," and Ball assented—the "I" would be referring to Desi.

The "Lucy" part of the title also grew out of the couple's personal life. Desi recalls:

> I started calling her "Lucy" shortly after we met; I didn't like the name "Lucille." That name had been used by other men. "Lucy" was mine alone. That's how, eventually, our television show was called I Love Lucy not "I Love Lucille."

The parts of Fred and Ethel Mertz were filled by William Frawley, an old character actor, and Vivian Vance, who was recommended by Marc Daniels, the young director chosen to supervise the first season of I Love Lucy. Ball was set to begin shooting, having recently been delivered of her first child—Lucie Desiree—in July.

On September 3, 1951 the four principal actors got together for the first time to read the script entitled "Lucy Thinks Ricky is Trying to Do Away with Her" while several dozen carpenters and electricians worked around them remodeling the building, installing the sets, and setting up Karl Freund's new lighting system. (Although this was the first segment shot, due to technical problems, the first episode to go out over the air was the second installment: "The Girls Want to Go to a Nightclub.")

On September 8, 1951, the audience filed in—and were almost thrown out when an inspector from the board of health failed to discover a separate washroom for the ladies. Ball casually offered her own dressing room; the Arnaz orchestra started playing; and the Cuban bandleader went out to warm up the audience. After all the starring players had been introduced and Ball blew kisses to the audience, Daniels instructed the actors to take their places, and the first episode of I Love Lucy began.

A scant six months, or twenty-six episodes later, it became the first television program to be seen in ten million homes—out of a total of only fifteen million sets in operation at the time. By April, I Love Lucy was the top program in the nation and the first-ranking program in almost every major city. Since every television set was estimated to reach 2.9 viewers, the show was seen by 30,740,000 individuals, nearly a fifth of the nation's population.

In 1952 the National Academy of Television Arts and Sciences gave Lucille Ball an Emmy for Best Comedienne and awarded Ball and Arnaz an Emmy for the Best Situation Comedy. In that same year, Ball became gave birth to her second child Desi, Jr. The show based seven episodes (supervised by a minister, priest, and rabbi) on Lucy Ricardo's on air "pregnancy" (without ever mentioning the word). When Lucy delivered "Little Ricky" in an episode called "Lucy Goes to the Hospital," 44 million viewers tuned in. Only 29 million watched Eisenhower's swearing in ceremony.

Even a McCarthy era accusation of being a Communist could not stick to America's favorite redheaded comedienne. Ball, who considered herself apolitical ("I haven't voted in years") had registered as a Communist to please her socialist grandfather and hadn't even voted in the election. When the truth was known, the committee dismissed the case after five days of scandal.

The early days of *I Love Lucy* were blissful. Ball and Arnaz used to turn down invitations to parties because nothing could match the fun they were having daily on the set. But, gradually, the marriage came under greater, and finally, insupportable stress. Instead of bringing the couple together, which was widely promoted as the virtual reason for its existence, upward mobility drove them apart. Whether it was the pressures of a weekly series, the stress of forced togetherness on a couple who were used to independent careers, Ball's overwhelming popularity and fame (people liked Ricky; they *loved* Lucy), Arnaz' escalating drinking and womanizing (reported by widespread gossip), or Ball's perfectionism, as *Lucy* provided the public with domestic romance, the Ball/Arnaz marriage fell apart.

The truth was carefully managed by public relations agents and even sanitized and served up as domestic comedy. (Ball's real jealousy over Arnaz's affairs provided comic fodder for an episode where Lucy and Ethel disguise themselves and go on a "blind date" with their husbands to trick them into infidelity.) But off-stage the Ball/Arnaz marriage continued to disintegrate. *I Love Lucy* went off the prime time schedule in 1960—the same year as the Arnaz/Ball divorce. (Ball subsequently married comedian Gary Morton, a little-publicized union that lasted over twenty years.)

After the divorce, Ball bought out Arnaz and continued on in a successful single-parent series. Ball starred in *The Lucy Show* 1962-68, and *Here's Lucy* 1968-74 (the latter two starring Ball's "Lucy" but minus Arnaz's "Ricky.") The later shows were well-crafted along the lines of *I Love Lucy*, but they never achieved its monumental popularity . In the 1980's, she began a new situation comedy as a grandmother that was quickly canceled and starred in a television movie *Stone Pillow*, where she played a bag lady.

The basic situation of *I Love Lucy* has become so well known as to form a kind of media folktale. Lucille Ball, the comedic center of the show, plays "Lucy Ricardo," a zany, red-headed housewife; Desi Arnaz, her real life husband, plays "Ricky Ricardo," Lucy's husband, a Cuban singer, bongo drummer, and band leader at the Tropicana nightclub. "Fred and Ethel Mertz," the Ricardos' neighbors, landlords, and best friends, are played by William Frawley and Vivian Vance. Many of the plots turn on Lucy's madcap schemes to get into show business despite Ricky's objections. In these, as well as in other escapades, Lucy often joins forces with Ethel as ally and confidante.

Simplified to their essential, farcical outlines, the Ricardos are a prototype of the odd couple; she is the kook, he is the exasperated, pragmatic straightman. The Mertzes are parental, less attractive figures who provide confidants and allies as the Ricardos enact their comedic battle of the sexes.

Vivian Vance was actually younger than Lucille Ball. It was written into her contract that she had to remain overweight and dress in frumpy clothes for the show—presumably to provide a less attractive foil for Lucy. Ball's glamorization was further enhanced by the constant presence of her make-up artist, Max Factor's brother-in-law, and by Freund's diffused lighting—taking her age down to the officially stated twenty-nine instead of Ball's over forty. By 1953, the success of the series encouraged them to hire award-winning Elois Jensen as her costumer.

None of this "glamor-girl" treatment ever surfaces in the series. On screen, Lucy is a naive madcap. But Ball, former model and Goldwyn Girl, knew the value of subliminal seduction, even in the role of a goofy housewife. Her outfits, attitude, and coiffeur combine domestic propriety, comic exaggeration, and respectable sexiness. She wears conventional shirtwaists, suits, and capri pants—all cut to reveal her statuesque figure—while she mugs or tosses a head full of improbably orange curls.

Ball's sexiness, part of her showgirl background, figured strongly in her vaudeville act. Ball regularly concluded the act by appearing onstage in a green split skirt with spangles and sequins. As a 1950 *Variety* review stated, "She pops the eyes out of the first row viewers with her hip-slinging activities to hyped beat of 'Cuban Pete.'" Lucy never does anything quite that provocative, although she occasionally wears revealing costumes, for example, an off-the-shoulder Italian peasant blouse and a cinch belt that accentuates her curves. The other characters respond to this by ignoring everything but her "big feet."

Lucy's most striking physical feature is her red hair, dyed during Ball's days as a Hollywood showgirl and contract player. Ball started out as a brunette, went blonde, and finally red in a desperate bid to stand out on the MGM lot. Red, the "hot" color, suggests excitement, sexual passion, and a temper—everything "hot-blooded." Red hair has adorned sexy, tempestuous, Hollywood glamour girls from Rita Hayworth to Ann-Margaret. Capitalizing on this connotation, the MGM publicity department released a story on the decision to dye Ball's then platinum hair: "The hair is blond but the soul, it is fire. We will dye the hair red."

Ball herself disclaims such high flown symbolism: "The story is ridiculous. Red was a happy color. It was good with my eyes, and it photographed well. It turned out to be a successful color. There's nothing more to it than that."

Once Ball began making a name for herself as a comic performer, her unruly orange hair began to suggest less the hot-blooded vamp and more the circus clown. Her cap of red curls became an emblem of Lucy's spunky optimism and cartoonish capers. Lucy's big, red-lipsticked mouth carries the same double message. Like her upswept hairdo, it is a carry over from the film fashions of the forties, when Ball was a minor player, and stars like Joan Crawford were made up with an over-drawn, scarlet lip line. On Lucy, the glamour lips, like the hairdo, are slightly clownish—a big, red, circus mouth that slides past its own sultriness into a dopey grin or a comedic, infantile howl.

Ball's big, blue, mascara-spiked eyes are another glamour plus. But again, Lucy exaggerates their effect for humor. She widens them into saucer-sized daffiness, careens her eyeballs in comic disbelief, goes bug-eyed with comic fear, or crosses her pupils to gain a better view of her own nose.

Eventually, these expressions and vocalisms became her trademarks and were written right into the scripts. The horrified "Spider Look" turns her face to jello. The "Light Bulb Look" pops her eyes into a thousand watts of astonishment. The "Credentials look" sets her jaw sagging in comic outrage. The "Gobloots Voice" turns a statuesque ex-showgirl into a quavering little girl lost. And who can forget her "Rickyyyyyy!"—that cross between a yelp and a foghorn that signals an oncoming tantrum?

The slapstick antics that are an important part of Lucy's appeal demand stamina and physical daring. Ball was tall and strong. As a showgirl she had to wear elaborate costumes, including huge head-pieces. Now she was ready to hold her own in rough-and-tumble physical comedy.

In one episode set in Italy, Lucy, who always wants to get into show business, is spotted by a film director. He doesn't mention that he sees her as a typical American tourist, and she fancies herself as the next Anna Magnani or Sophia Loren, playing an Italian peasant in a movie called *Bitter Grapes*.

To prepare herself for her role, she visits a winery to soak up some local color. Outfitted in a "peasant" costume, she is mistaken for one of the workers. The supervisor orders her to climb into a large, wooden wine vat with a real peasant. At first, she imitates the other woman's brisk efficiency in stomping the grapes. But utilitarian, adult behavior bores Lucy, and she soon pulls her co-worker into a mock tarantella. When the other woman demands that Lucy actually work, the redheaded comedienne tries to leave. The peasant insists, and they become involved in a comic battle— smashing grapes in each other's face and wrestling in the bottom of the vat among the squashed grapes and wine.

Apparently, the local color was all too real. "Those grapes were like stepping on eyeballs!" exclaims Ball. "And they got a real Italian peasant who didn't speak English, and she wouldn't let me up!"

The sight of Ball in her off-the-shoulder, peasant outfit winding up in a grape-wrestling bout is one of the classic comedy bits from *I Love Lucy*. Desi Arnaz, in his own autobiography felt that such scenes are not only hilarious, but sexy—like the comedy of Carole Lombard, Ball's favorite actress:

> Carole had a quality which is rare; you can count the women who have had it on the fingers of one hand. Carole, while doing the antics of a clown, disheveled,rain-soaked, disregarding how she looked even with mud all over her, could make you laugh, and yet at the same time, make you want to go to bed with her. Lucy has that same quality.

Whatever sexiness existed was underplayed in the television series. If audiences responded to Ball's sexiness, it was as a kind of "feminine" sizzle over the whole farcical proceedings. What showed up again and again in the numerous letters and calls that flooded the show was a delight in the "Lucy/Ricky romance" and her conse-quent "femininity." As Ball remembers:

Our audience were happy that I hadn't lost my femininity. That was because Ricky and Lucy were in love. They never got truly angry—only comedically angry. There was always a happy ending.

Ball's sexiness—she had, after all, made her initial success playing tough, glamour girls—lingered on in *I Love Lucy* as a subtle subtext—an unacknowledged bonus to the slapstick antics and domestic romance. Her vaudeville act may have included some hip-slinging in a spangled, sequined split skirt, but as Lucy, she confined herself to modest, domestic outfits that only hint at her curvaceous figure.

Lucy's look was typical of the female heroines on television situation comedies of the 1950's. Margaret Anderson of *Father Knows Best*, Gracie of *The George Burns and Gracie Allen Show*, Miss Brooks, spinster schoolteacher of *Our Miss Brooks*, and even Alice Kramden,who kissed and made up with her corpulent bus driver husband Ralph on *The Honeymooners*, all had trim, youthful figures, set off by neat shirtwaist dresses. We had to wait until the 1970's for *All in the Family* to bring us Edith Bunker, who was middle aged and looked it, and until the 1980's to bring us *Roseanne*, a working class housewife who is overweight, overworked, and fond of dressing in loose sweats—like many of her viewers.

Lucy Ricardo, like other 1950's sitcom housewives was made up and costumed to look appealing but scripted and directed to never be consciously seductive. The notion of Lucy's being sexually aggressive (not merely affectionate), even toward her husband, is played for laughs. In one episode, "The Girls Want to Go to a Nightclub," Lucy and Ethel discover that their husbands have arranged blind dates for themselves. To ward off marital straying, Lucy and Ethel dress up as hillbillies and show up as their husbands' dates. Outfitted as homely bumpkins, Lucy and Ethel make plays for their husbands and chase the dumbfounded men around the room. Once the husbands discover who they are, they in turn chase the wives. Now that there may be some real consequences to their aggression, the women retreat.

Both her silly costume and her schoolyard, tomboyish chasing after her husband mock the idea that Lucy might be a mature, seductive woman. Ball's showgirl sex appeal was tamed and made respectable for Lucy's domestic audience. As Ball states:

I never got letters from fans saying that I was sexy. But they would write saying that they were glad that I hadn't lost my femininity.

Femininity was an important part of Lucy's persona—even in the midst of the wildest slapstick. Lucille Ball contrasts her own style with that of other physical comediennes.

Some of them did outrageous things that were laughed at mostly by men. Martha Raye, especially, because she played a lot to the army boys. She'd do these crazy, kind of suggestive things, and do them with a flair that was funny and accepted. And Joan Davis was another kind of mugger. She did a lot of mugging and straddling—her legs were always like this. (Ball sprawls open-legged on the elegant chair.) It wasn't always ladylike. But she had a flair of a different kind and vitality. I have no wish to mug or be too masculine. I can mug, I can scream, I can smoke a cigar. But I have to have a very strong story reason to do it. I can play an old, drunken bag lady, always swiggin' gin, and I have a ball. But I'm not gross.

The sense that Lucy is essentially a lady mirrored the values of her domestic audience and suited the genre of 1950's situation comedy. *I Love Lucy* was broadcast into people's living rooms once a week. It was the era of one television set per household and limited program selection; and housewives controlled the tv dial. The nuclear family was idealized as the source of human contentment, and there was a low divorce rate. Television portrayed single women like Miss Brooks as virginal spinsters chasing confirmed bachelors; and homosexuality was invisible. The Lucy/Desi romance gave a sweet, comforting buzz to a situation comedy cocktail of domesticity and slapstick comedy.

Just as Lucy's respectable attractiveness is a tame version of Ball's showgirl sensuality, her fruitless attempts to get into Ricky's nightclub act is a sharply scaled-down version of Ball's show business ambitions. Like her sexiness, Ball's professional success would probably have been threatening to a domestic audience. But Lucy is never threatening. She is endearingly untalented and naive. Her imaginative, funny schemes are what many housewives, longing for a more glamourous way of life and trapped by their own limitations, would love to do.

Just as Lucy's career ambitions are ridiculous, her education is limited. Like most of the 1950's housewives in her audience, she appears to lack a college degree or any sort of professional training. Despite Lucille Ball's remarkable achievements as a comedienne, Lucy Ricardo supposedly has no particular talent for performing. She doesn't sing, dance, or act. In fact, she fulfills the early assessment of Ball's talent, when she was told that as a showgirl, she didn't have the ability to even walk across a stage! But while Ball's beauty, drive, willingness to learn, and comedic talent eventually led to fame and fortune, Lucy Ricardo's hapless efforts lead only to laughs.

Many episodes turn on the premise that Lucy is comically inept when she tries to imitate the skills of her artistic betters, particularly when she tries to get into Ricky's act. As a ballerina, she hangs upside down from the ballet barre. As a showgirl, she stumbles down a grand staircase, headdress slipping over her eyes. In her most famous bit, as the "Vitameatavegamin Girl" in a television commercial, she gets drunk.

The only thing she is good at is being a housewife and consumer. Lucy and Ethel covet washers, dryers, freezers, Cadillacs, and fur coats. Their shopping sprees are guilty pleasures. Without income of their own, they are always in danger of overspending their husbands' money and causing a domestic quarrel. In one episode. "Ricky Loses His Temper," Lucy loses a bet that she can control her compulsive shopping. She can't—but neither can he keep his temper.

The Ricardo's upward mobility mirrored the post-War economic boom and the many advertisements for new products and travel. As the series progressed, the Ricardos move to an apartment with a window, buy a car (which Lucy—the quintessential "female driver"—crashes), travel cross-country to Hollywood, stay in a deluxe hotel suite, and move to suburban Connecticut. In one of the funniest episodes "Lucy Does the Tango," Lucy, now an entrepreneurial chicken farmer, stuffs her clothing with eggs and dances with Ricky. They collide, smashing the eggs, and a concealed door slams into Ethel,who has also stuffed her dress with eggs. The trashing of possessions, a classic farce device, suggests that as desirable as they may be, they, and the middle class lifestyle they represent, are ultimately oppressive and easily demolished by Lucy's infantile,comic anarchy.

In fact, the entire series conveys this double message. Lucy Ricardo is an upwardly mobile, middle class housewife and mother, the 1950's pre-feminist ideal. She was a competent homemaker, cook, and loving wife and mother. No matter how zany her schemes, they never involve any risk to her television child or household.

She is also frustrated, bored, and (comedically) angry. Her efforts to get into Ricky's act is her rebellion at her confinement to the domestic sphere. In "The Ballet" she announces "Here I am with all this talent bottled up inside me, and you're sitting on the cork.... I'm going to get into that show or my name's not Lucy Ricardo!" Her anger at Ricky for confining her ("Ricky has kept me from becoming a famous actress") results in her trying to upstage him by stealing his screen test and even pulling off his pants.

In another episode, Lucy trains to be a burlesque clown. Every time she says the name "Martha," she is hit with a pig bladder, sprayed with seltzer, and gets a pie in the face. She vows that next time she does the sketch, she will reverse roles and "get even." She dons male clown clothing and heads for Ricky's nightclub trying to get into his act and programmed to retaliate when she hears "Martha." Ricky croons a romantic Spanish ballad to "Martha," and Lucy leaps onstage, beats the male ballet dancers with a pig's bladder, squirts the ballerina with seltzer, and hits the tuxedoed Ricky in the face with a pie. (The Saudi Arabian government reacted to the comic subversion of male authority by banning the series.)

Here on the domestic front, it's possible that Lucy's insubordination was made more palatable by a subtle kind of racism. Ricky's Cuban accent (constantly mimicked by Lucy), his incomplete grasp of the English language, and his dark and handsome "Latin lover" persona may have made his humiliation by All-American Lucy acceptable. (Remember, the CBS executives didn't even want him on the show.) By way of contrast, note *The George Burns and Gracie Allen Show* (his name first) a contemporary situation comedy starring another dizzy housewife who gets the best of her husband. *Burns and Allen* is told from the point of view of the native English speaker George. Although befuddled by Gracie, he is never physically humiliated. In any case, Gracie was a verbal, not a physical comedienne— and physical comedy has traditionally been a male prerogative (with rare exceptions like Lucille Ball and Carol Burnett.) And where many of the *Lucy* shows end with "now we're even" *Burns and Allen* ends with his instructing her to "Say good night, Gracie."

But no matter how often Lucy said, "we're even," dependent housewives weren't and aren't. Lucy's fantastic schemes to get into show business echoed the frustrations and fantasies of millions of housewives. The domestic malaise of the 1950's, which Betty Friedan charted in *The Feminine Mystique*, surfaces in a disguised, comedic form in *I Love Lucy*, as Lucy revolts against the tedium of being Mrs. Ricardo. Her vaudeville turns and comic inventiveness made the repression and boredom of domesticity bearable and helped her viewers sidestep the real issues with laughter.

In fact, all of Lucy's efforts to escape the feminine, domestic sphere are portrayed as ridiculous inept. In one episode, Lucy attempts to prove that she is capable of "bringing home the bacon" by switching jobs with Ricky for a week. When she goes to an employment agency, her interviewer discovers that she has no skills, except for making candy (a domestic activity), and assigns her and pal Ethel to a candy factory. As a candy dipper, Lucy winds up in a chocolate fight. When she and Ethel are told to wrap candies as they move along a conveyor belt, they are unable to keep up with the swiftly moving contraption, and wind up stuffing candies in their mouths, hats, blouses, etc. The husbands turn out to be equally incapable in the domestic sphere, so each sex returns to its gender-proper role.

Gender stereotyping provides humor in the show. Fred is grumpy, Ethel overeats, Lucy shops, Ricky explodes, Lucy and Ethel are nosy (Fred calls them the "snooper patrol") and emotive, while Ricky and Fred want to "be the boss" (which Lucy's schemes undermine).

If Ricky is the would-be parental figure, Lucy is childlike. She is gullible and naive, believing both the best (that she is about to star in an Italian movie) and the worst (that Ricky is planning to do away with her) on minimal evidence. Her lack of adult common sense provides the springboard for elaborate, imaginative, funny schemes. She dresses in costume, engages in trickery, and sneaks into movie stars' homes, nightclubs, and all sorts of fascinating places! Her schemes fail to achieve a real show business career—returning Lucy to her secure, if stifling, domestic nest. If Lucy fails on a permanent narrative level, she succeeds brilliantly in manipulating others (especially Ethel) to reach her ends and entertaining her audience with her comic antics.

Lucy's schemes create the farcical mid-section that is the heart of the show. Framing this funny, fantastic mid-section is a beginning and end set in the mundane reality of the Ricardo's middle-class existence. In the realistic "frame" of each episode, Lucy seems to accomplish little or nothing. She does not get hired at the candy factory. She does not get Ricky to take her to a nightclub. She does not get into show business, whether as an Italian movie star, a "Vitameatavegamin Girl," or a ballet dancer.

What she does do is create an atmosphere of fun to surmount the tedium of married life. She also amuses and maintains the ultimately adoring interest of her husband. She manages, at least temporarily, to convince others to go along with her schemes and pay enormous attention to her. The theme of the show is summed up in its title: *I Love Lucy*.

Lucy's lovability is crucial to the success of the program. Her manipulation is confined to innocent, absurd goals. In our interview, Ball was incensed by any suggestion that Lucy was devious.

If Lucy is manipulative, she is only childishly so. How she's going to tell Ricky she's going to pay back thirty-two dollars—not big murders like you see today on the soaps. Childlike is small matters and white lies. We got tons of letters from people saying they'd love to be able to manipulate their lives the way Lucy does!

As a character, Lucy is a paradox. She is innocent and manipulative, foolish and clever, an ordinary housewife and an extraordinary farceur. In the realistic section of the plot, her intellect seems average, even childishly subnormal—a blend of gullibility, emotionality, and impulsiveness. In the imaginative mid-section of each episode she becomes brilliant, concocting elaborate schemes to further her ends...." If Lucy's schemes for ambition and fame narratively failed, with the result that she was held, often gratefully, to domesticity (and Ricky was therefore right) performatively they succeeded." She never manages to change her situation, but she entertains brilliantly.

Lucy's multi-layers are perfectly suited to a zany domestic situation comedy. Her ordinary side creates identification with the average housewife and grounds her character in reality. Her childishness motivates her to go for what she wants—no matter how absurd. Her brilliance creates the entertaining stratagems of each episode. Because her creative intelligence operates only in that mid-section, she does not change her status in the course of any single episode. At the end of each episode, things return to the status quo—the essentially unchanging situation which is crucial to the genre of the situation comedy.

Situation comedy, while it derived some of its format from radio, vaudeville, and silent movies, really came of age with the advent of television and particularly with the phenomenal success of *I Love Lucy*. Basically, a situation comedy consists of a twenty-six minute playlet in which characters get themselves into scrapes and out again. The characters tend to be written in terms of broad, clear behaviors and dialogue. The audience quickly grasps who these characters are. With no need to devote stage time to exploring murky, psychological depths, the bulk of the twenty-six minutes can be devoted to funny action and easily resolved problems. Since the format is episodic, the audience tunes in to see the same characters in similar situations every week. Therefore, the characters must be basically lovable, no matter what their idiosyncrasies. They also tend to be domestic and middle-class. The central character or at least co-star in situation comedies is often a woman. David Poltrak, Vice-President of CBS Television, says: "Situation comedies attract mainly a family audience, with a bias toward female viewers." Lucy, a broadly drawn, endearingly funny housewife, was an ideal heroine for a 1950's situation comedy. She was physically funny without being gross or crude; imaginative and innocently daring without being realistically competent; and attractive without being sexy. Her female viewers do not have to fear her as a competitor for their husbands' attention; nor does she raise uncomfortable sexual issues in the family living room. Instead, her attractiveness sweetens the Lucy/Desi battle of the sexes (many episodes end with "now we're even") with the Lucy/Desi romance. Lucy's competence splits along gender lines prescribed by 1950's sex roles. She is competent in the feminine domestic sphere and absurdly incompetent in the masculine sphere of work outside the home. Intellectually and emotionally, she embodies other feminine stereotypes: she is gullible, excitable, childlike, and manipulative (although in a harmless way.)

In fact, Lucy's position as a powerless housewife who moves the plot through her comedic manipulations is a modern variation of a theatrical type—the scheming servant. The comedically clever slave dates back over two thousand years to ancient Greek and Roman theatre. The commedia dell'arte (popular from the sixteenth through the eighteenth centuries) was full of comedic servants—the zanni. Shakespeare and Moliere (who based some of their plots on ancient sources and commedia dell'arte) also utilized the type. The tradition continued in varying forms wherever the social structure supported a master/servant relationship.

In contemporary American middle-class society, the domestic servant is the exception. His/her place has been taken by the housewife. Like the traditional servant, the housewife is economically and socially dependent on the male head of household. Rather than risk direct confrontation, she may feel that she is more likely to gain her ends through clever manipulation. The result is a tangled, amusing plot based on misunderstanding: a staple of situation comedy.

The I Love Lucy episodes may have a deeper source for their continuing appeal. According to Freudian theory, what makes us laugh is the sudden, pleasurable release of sexual and aggressive impulses in a disguised, palatable form. Lucy's sexual and aggressive impulses are masked and portrayed as innocent and funny. When she dresses in an Italian "peasant" outfit that features an off-the-shoulder blouse and a wide belt that accentuates her curves and has a wrestling match in a vat of grapes—we are meant to take it as amusing. But without the situation comedy format and Lucy's innocent, fun personality, the scene might look like today's controversial mud-wrestling matches—where half-naked women try to pin each other down in the mud for the amusement of mainly male spectators. When Lucy "accidentally" dumps a plate of spaghetti over the head of a male movie star who ignores her, we are meant to think it's funny—not angry. When, disguised as a hillbilly, she pursues Ricky around the bedroom, we are meant to take it as a farcical mix-up, not sexual aggression.

Minus the comic frame, Lucy's revolt against Ricky's control might suggest frustration; her upstaging him might indicate hostility; her jealousy over the gorgeous singers and dancers in his act might hint at insecurity; and even the Vitameatavegamin commercial might allude to the dangers of alcohol. None of this, of course, surfaces in *I Love Lucy*.

But in fact, the real Ball/Arnaz marriage was torn apart by some very serious problems. The Lucy/Desi battle of the sexes was a romantic comedy version of the Ball/Arnaz battle for control between a strong-willed Hollywood star and her less-famous, Latin, macho husband.

Ricky's flirtations may have been figments of Lucy's imagination, but Arnaz was a compulsive womanizer. Even Lucy's drunkenness in the Vitameatavegamin commercial was a light-hearted reversal of the true situation—Arnaz's alcoholism.

None of this intrudes on the Lucy/Ricky Ricardo television romance. Lucy's rebellion is treated as cute. Her efforts to undermine his authority, potentially embarrass him, and jeopardize his career are viewed as endearing. His annoyance is simply masculine stuffiness. Ball comments about the role of anger on *I Love Lucy*:

> No one on the show ever got really angry—only comedically angry. Once a guest star played real anger, and we had to stop him—it wasn't funny.

To underscore the idea that "it's all in fun," *I Love Lucy* frames the events with emblems of playfulness. The opening credits feature a cartoon heart with caricature drawings of the characters underscored by light-hearted music. The punched up, comic style of acting and a laugh track let us know that we are meant to be amused. In fact, after a few moments of watching *I Love Lucy* or similar programs, the viewer usually realizes that they are a situation comedy by the acting style alone.

It's a psychological truism that suppressed sexual and aggressive impulses are often released in dreams. *I Love Lucy* is structured so that we begin with reality, move into a long dream, and wake up to reality. The beginning of each episode anchors the viewer in the ordinary, middle-class lives of the Ricardos and their neighbors, the Mertzes.

From this mundane reality, we move into a dream, usually based on Lucy's exaggerated, emotional impulse. She concocts plans that pull us into a chain of farcical events. Six foot loaves of bread pop out of ovens; chocolates race by with supersonic speed; people wear absurd disguises and are not recognized.

Lucy's outrageous schemes operate with the same absurd logic as dreams. She can treat a cheese like a baby, and everyone else believes her because they are part of the same comedic dream. Realistic probabilities simply do not apply. In a dream, wishes and fears are exaggerated, treated as literally true, and acted upon. An ordinary housewife may worry that her husband is hostile to her. Lucy imagines that Ricky is trying to murder her. Following her absurd premise is her absurd reaction—she fortifies herself with a garbage can lid.

At the end of each dream-farce, Lucy wakes up. We return to the ordinary reality of the Ricardo's lives. No matter how outrageous Lucy's behavior, it has no consequences in the real world. She has only play-acted her childish fantasies, and "Daddy/Ricky" indulges and forgives her. The Ricardos and their viewers have an unspoken understanding: Ricky is in charge of reality; Lucy is in charge of fantasy. The structure of each episode allows Lucy to be both a respectable, beloved housewife and mother (in the opening and closing sections that frame each episode) and an anarchistic, infantile clown (in the farcical, dreamlike mid-section). Each episode ends as the two sections of a cartoon heart close to form a valentine, reminding millions of viewers to tune in next week for a satisfying mix of fantastic farce and domestic sentiment.

The astounding success of I Love Lucy derives from a combination of the right vehicle (domestic physical farce) with the right performer (Lucille Ball) and the Ball/Arnaz chemistry, plus the creative talent of the writers and directors, and the technological innovation and business acuity of Arnaz.

Another key factor in the success of the program was the emergence of television, the mass medium that permeated American homes with undreamed of speed. This medium found in I Love Lucy a program that could subliminally express the domestic discontents of its culture even as it masked and released them with laughter.

On a personal level, the Ball/Arnaz romance and fun that fueled the series disintegrated and ultimately led to their divorce—but not before their union successfully challenged notions of what was ethnically acceptable in a marriage, not before it gave them two children, and not before it gave the rest of us their brainchild—*I Love Lucy*. Ball and Arnaz knew what we all know—that relationships are often problematic and painful. *I Love Lucy* gives us respite from that knowledge. For twenty-six minutes (plus commercials), we take a family vacation. We tune out the difficulties and dullness of daily living and tune in a dream of domestic bliss and a deluge of laughter.

Sources

Andrews, Bart, *Lucy & Ricky & Fred & Ethel: The Story of I Love Lucy*, (New York: Fawcett Popular Library, 1976), p.192.

Andrews, Bart and Watson, Thomas J., *Loving Lucy*, (New York: Saint Martin's Press: 1980) p.121.

Arnaz, Desi, *A Book*, (New York: Warner Books, 1976) pp.185, 175, 121.

Ball, Lucille, personal interview conducted in her home in New York, New York, April 14, 1984.

Ball, Lucille, printed record of seminar sponsored by the American Film Institute, Los Angeles, California, June 12, 1972 .

Hirshberg, Lynn, "I Love Lucy" *Rolling Stone*, June 23, 1983, p.31.

Horowitz, Susan "Sitcom Domesticus: A Species Endangered by Social Change," *Television: The Critical View*, fourth edition, Edited by Horace Newcomb (New York, Oxford: Oxford University Press, 1987), Reprinted from Channels Magazine, Vol X, Sept./Oct., 1984,

Mellencamp, Patrica, *High Anxiety: Catastrophe, Scandal, Age, & Comedy*, (Bloomington and Indianapolis: Indiana University Press, 1992) pp.328, 329.

Phyllis Diller

Phyllis Diller trots onto a nightclub stage dressed in a *Mad Magazine* version of an evening gown. Silver lamé is bunched into knee length ruffles, while the rest of the costume puffs out to imply a Humpty Dumpty body. Under her armpits, more lamé sags like a glitzy trash can liner and finishes in ruffles at the wrists. A blue satin bodice balloons skyward toward padded, pointy shoulders. Diller seems to be not so much dressed as upholstered into the semblance of a shiny, stuffed toy.

Accessorizing the costume are gloves, a cartoon-length cigarette holder, and a king-sized cigarette. "The cigarette is made of wood," says Diller. "I don't smoke."

Her coiffure is as artificial as the cigarette, being comprised of a fright wig of platinum Dynel. Years ago, Diller went to a scalp specialist because her hair was falling out. The specialist advised her to use a curry comb to stimulate hair growth. The treatment worked, but it made her hair stand up. One night, she went onstage that way, the audience roared, and she kept the hairdo—incorporating the coiffure into its present electric shock style.

In this outlandish get-up, the comic's actual facial features are hardly noticeable. The nightclub crowd, who greet her appearance with raucous laughter, sees only an absurd harridan—not (after several well-publicized episodes of plastic surgery) a delicately pretty, gently aging lady. This lady, with large green eyes and pale pink lipstick greets me in her hotel suite wearing a flattering, floor-length robe made of elegant squirrel skin. But as Miss Diller points out, "Elegance and beauty are not funny."

Nor did they—or the financial ease that paid for them—come easy. At the age of thirty-seven, Diller (born Phyllis Driver in 1917) was a housewife, the mother of five children, and the spouse of a failed businessman. Prodded by her husband, Sherwood Diller, and equipped only with a sense of humor and the necessity of providing for her children, Diller set out to become a stand-up comic—a profession in which women were practically non-existent. Miss Diller notes dryly: "They had no idea what I was. It was like—'Get a stick and kill it before it multiplies!'"

However, after an initial struggle, Diller met with her first real success at San Francisco's Purple Onion in 1955, where she was booked for two weeks and stayed for eighty-nine. Since then, she has enjoyed an active career as a headliner for almost forty years. She has starred in three television series, including *The Pruitts of Southampton,* and numerous specials. She has appeared in thirteen feature films and co-starred in three comedies with Bob Hope, whom she accompanied on his Christmas jaunts to Vietnam. She starred in numerous other plays and musicals, including *Hello, Dolly* on Broadway. She has recorded several comedy albums and published four best selling comedy books—*Phyllis Diller's Housekeeping Hints, Phyllis Diller's Marriage Manual, The Complete Mother,* and, most recently, *The Joys of Aging and How to Avoid Them.* Originally trained as a classical musician, she has appeared as a piano soloist with 100 symphony orchestras playing Beethoven and Bach under the name Dame Illya Dillya.

First and foremost, she is a stand-up comic, playing large hotels such as Caesar's Palace in Las Vegas, the Waldorf Astoria in New York, and the Tropicana in Atlantic City. Her popularity and longevity as a performer testify to both uncommon wit and perseverance. In an interview in *The New York Post,* she commented that she went on the old Jack Paar *Tonight Show* fifty times before anyone knew who she was. "When I was on ten times nobody knew my name. After twenty times they thought I was Florence Dillon. Thirty times I was that blonde with five kids. Rome was not built in a day! Ah-ha-ha-ha!"

"That blond" is a decidedly oddball version of a housewife. Diller has called her onstage character an "idiot" and a "harridan," and is bemused by the tendency of audiences to confuse her person with her act. In fact, the refined, sensitive woman who greets me in her hotel suite seems to have little in common with the cartoon virago that has just kept a gambling hotel audience in an uproar. One of few things that linger off-stage is the laugh—a good-humored cackle that erupts into an infectious, unladylike guffaw. The laugh is a Diller original ("I've always had it") and regularly punctuates our interview. She laughs easily, generously, as much at someone else's jokes as at her own. But however spontaneous the origin of her humor, by the time the Diller comedy style reaches the stage, it is carefully honed and polished. The result is a rapid-fire, meticulously timed series of one-liners.

Diller's cockeyed comments, comedic cackle, and funny-ugly appearance add up to an onstage personality that is both simpler and larger than life. She has created her onstage self as a kind of trade-marked character like "Broomhilda the Witch," the cartoon heroine of a syndicated comic strip. (Marilyn Monroe, another blonde who achieved celebrity in the 1950's, acted out a flipside version of the same process. Born Norma Jean Baker and brunette, Monroe's image was bleached of all complexity and inflated into a blonde bombshell. That pneumatic image, mega-famous during her lifetime, is still being marketed, years after her death, as a trademark to sell every-thing from bath towels to ashtrays.)

Diller's onstage appearance, like the content of her act, evolved gradually. In her early act, Diller did impressions—the Dean of Women in a jabot and pince-nez or Jeannette McDonald in a fluffy stole and flowered hat, and performed her comedy from the crook of a grand piano.

> In those days there were two shows, *The Ed Sullivan Show* and the the Jack Paar *Tonight Show*. I was a big hit on the Jack Paar *Tonight Show,* and that was for scale. Now you understand, I had a family to sup-port. *The Ed Sullivan Show* was for a lot of money for the same thing—also it was prestigious. My goal was to get on *The Ed Sullivan Show.* My thought was: "When you see a comic on that show, he always works in front of a bare curtain."...I knew that I had to get rid of props....That's when I started becoming commercial. And I did get the Sullivan Show.

The visual carryover from the props in Diller's early act are her flamboyantly ugly costumes. The costumes evolved gradually. Orig-inally Diller used a great variety of props, which she abandoned for the sake of greater commercial appeal. But she was outfitted in nor-mal, even chic clothes.

> I had a Balmain. It was the cocktail suit of the year—in *Vogue* and *Bazaar.* It had big flat buttons in front, and it was quite chic. And I said,

"You can twist these knobs all night, and the picture doesn't get any better!"

This kind of remark is, of course, an example of the kind of self-deprecating humor with which Diller is identified. The main source of her supposed inadequacy is her lack of sex appeal. Diller is not simply plain or sexually neutral. She is aggressively, comedically repellent—her sexual charms are absurdly inferior to those of any member of her audience.

Her costume of ballooning lamé illustrates her words. The outfit is grotesque, unflattering, and funny. It emphasizes her skinny legs and implies an oddly shaped torso. Even before she opens her mouth, her appearance mocks the very notion of feminine appeal. Unattractiveness is raised to a level of surrealism—no woman in the real world dresses in a lamé version of the Queen of Clubs.

Diller's verbal self-abuse is just as surreal:

The hair on the top of my head is so thin, the part is on the roof of my mouth.

On my honeymoon I put on a peekaboo blouse. My husband peeked and booed.

Her raucous laugh, which regularly punctuates her lines, assures us that what might sound like a painful lack of sexual self-confidence is really all in fun.

The artificiality of Diller's stand-up character is underscored by a seeming paradox. Diller herself has undergone major plastic surgery and several facelifts. As a result, she now has regular, pleasant features and looks quite attractive. Diller's plastic surgery gave an enormous boost to her career. She was one of the first celebrities to speak frankly about face-lifts and benefited from the shock and curiosity value. She was also simply prettier—and that makes for a more attractive stage presence and photographs.

But her remodeled, pretty features in no way detract from her onstage "ugliness." Her supposed repulsiveness remains a workable comic premise, especially since she performs on a nightclub stage at some distance from her audience. The subtle changes in her features are overshadowed by her frightwig and odd costumes. (The revealing close-ups of film and television are less amenable to this sort of artificial premise.) But Diller's nightclub audience is ready to believe that she has both undergone plastic surgery to improve her appearance and that she is irredeemably ugly. In fact, she regularly refers to the surgery in her act. To help her audience bridge the paradox,

Diller emphasizes not her beautification, but her extreme need that led to the operations:

> I had to do something. I had so many wrinkles, I could screw my hats on.

Some younger female comics disdain this kind of self-deprecating material, but Diller refuses to worry about whether her material could be construed as anti-feminist or demeaning to women:

> I care about my career and my work—whatever makes people laugh. I'm not trying to make any point. My feeling about life has nothing to do with my work onstage. I don't care if it's anti-feminist. I don't know what that means. I want to be funny and get as many laughs as possible, and I do it however I can without bad taste. The young girls are into women's lib and the ERA—I don't want a message onstage. I may offend them. I know I have offended some. But I can't let that affect my work.

Self-deprecation is, of course, a time-honored tool for stand-up comics. The original comics were court jesters, low-status "fools" who were given license to twit their betters. Today's successful stand-ups usually let us know by their words or behavior that they are, somehow, inadequate. Rodney Dangerfield moans, "I don't get no respect." Woody Allen slumps and shrugs haplessly at his misfortunes. Joan Rivers denounces her "fat" thighs. Some moan about their difficulties with relationships and the impossibility of finding dates and marriage partners. Others stutter, mispronounce words, giggle nervously, or dress in ill-fitting clothes. Says Diller:

> I find it charming. It's not necessary, but it's a lot harder to do without self-deprecation. It endears you to the audience. It makes you seem—look, I'm not such hot stuff, I'm just one of you guys. I'm not perfect....If some of the girls did it, they would get further faster. It's a great way to say hello. The only way to learn comedy is in front of the audience—which is humiliating. When I started out, I didn't know how to say hello to an audience. And to this day, my hello relates to something I am wearing.

In keeping with Diller's persona as the negation of traditionally desirable feminine traits, she is not only inept as a sex object, she is hopeless as a housewife.

> Of course, I should never have gotten married to anybody. I hate housekeeping. I don't like to do it, and I just don't do it. Hell, we've got a ring around the tub you can set a drink on.

The house is full of bugs. I wear a flea collar around both ankles. There isn't a person in our family that's got the guts to eat raisin toast.

I just have trouble with my cooking. Damn it! Our vet told us that because of my cooking our cat has only two lives left.

Phyllis Diller came out of the 1950's, a period which stressed and exaggerated sex-role differences. It was the time of Marilyn Monroe (all bosom, blondness, and baby-voice) and Margaret Anderson (the all-understanding wife and mother of *Father Knows Best*.) The ideal woman was irresistibly seductive and/or chastely domestic. But Diller and Rivers comedically counterpointed the image of woman as harlot/housewife by wisecracking about their sexual and domestic defects. Interestingly, in light of their failure at these aspects of the female role, neither comic presents herself as an inadequate or hostile mother. The closest Diller gets are remarks about overdoing motherhood.

We had far too many kids. At one time in our playpen it was standing room only. It looked like a bus stop for midgets.

But neither Diller nor Rivers displays any resentment, even comedically, toward particular children, perhaps because audiences tend to identify the stand-up act with the performer. The confusion is almost inevitable—for one thing, the performer and the on-stage character have the same name. Portraying oneself as a "bad mother," even comically, may be too unsympathetic to be funny.

Like the stand-up comic, an actress in a long-term situation comedy tends to be identified with her role. People think of Lucille Ball as "Lucy Ricardo," who was always a loving, competent mother (no matter how dizzy she acted otherwise).

Sketch characters and dramatic roles, on the other hand, are clearly "acted." Their costumes, circumstances, and attitudes belong to roles that the actress can leave behind. Carol Burnett can play "Eunice" and "Miss Hannigan" as child-hating harridans. "Eunice" can call her unwanted sons "no-neck monsters," and no one wonders if Carol Burnett hates children.

But stand-up comics walk a thinner line between autobiography and fiction. Perhaps an abusive mother—even in jest—is just not funny. A mother is overwhelmingly powerful in relation to her helpless children. And it is with the comedically victimized child that Diller comedically identifies.

I was the world's ugliest baby. I have photos of my folks leaving the hospital with sacks over their heads.

I was thirty years old. My mother was still trying to get an abortion!

I asked my mother how to turn off the electric fan. She said, "Grab the blade!"

The comic victim is a universal type, Many of Diller's jokes, such as the one about the electric fan, can be told by either a female or male comic. Shakespeare's plays are full of luckless, lower-class bumpkins and servants—as are the Italian commedia dell'arte and the comedies of Moliere.

Yiddish humor is particularly rich in funny unfortunates—*schlemiels* and *schlimazls*—who are portrayed with affection and amused contempt, In fact, Diller presents herself as a kind of wise-cracking, WASP *schlimazl.* Her self-deprecating, female humor gives her an outsider's vulnerability missing from the insider persona of WASP males like Bob Hope and Johnny Carson, but present in many Jewish male comics like Woody Allen and Rodney Dangerfield.

Like the *schlimazl's* woes, Diller's "ugliness" is meant to arouse laughter, not tears. Diller's on-stage persona—the unattractive, budget-conscious housewife decked out in bizarre costumes and wigs—allows her audience to identify with, condescend to, and laugh at her—without guilt. Since she verbally and visually ridicules her siuation, so can we.

Diller's onstage character came out of her own home situation. Diller was a middle-aged mother of five with a husband who was a failed businessman. Today, Diller is a Hollywood star. She lives in a twenty-two room mansion, cooks gourmet meals, dresses with taste and elegance, and has boyfriends. None of this surfaces in her act. The act is, as Diller puts it, "Frozen. Like Jack Benny never became generous. His premise was that he was stingy. I have my premise." The on-stage Diller is in the same boat—in fact a leakier one—than her audience. Similarly, "Lucy and Ricky Ricardo" continued to cope with economic problems which had long ceased to trouble the wealthy Ball and Arnaz.

"Lucy Ricardo" existed within the framework of the situation comedy, complete with sets, other characters, dialogue, action, and an episodic, comedic plot. Diller's character exists alone on a night-club stage. She alone must create, by means of her words and gestures, an imaginary comedic world, with herself at the center. All stand-up comics must get the audience to buy into their particular angle on reality. Diller does so by verbally creating a cast of fantasy characters that she has incorporated into her act. Preeminent among those characters is "Fang," her onstage husband.

You wouldn't believe how cheap this man is! We just had an anniversary. Dinner was going great until the tray fell off the car.

Course he is the stupidest man alive! There's no doubt about it. He went up to a thermostat. He said, "Seventy! My God! I've lost ninety pounds!"

He hates work. One day he called in dead.

It's close to the truth because of the way he boozes. He had an honorable mention in the obituary column eight times.

When we went to bed together it's a case of the naked and the dead.

Fang is a composite of the worst traits of all husbands. He is cheap, stupid, lazy, drunk, and sexually indifferent. Compared to Diller's marital situation, any woman in the audience has it good—and can imaginatively vent a little hostility besides. And the men don't have to take offense because "Fang" is so clearly a cartoon exaggeration. In the light of theories of comedy as disguised anger, it is interesting to note Diller's comment on her own use of anger:

> The first guy I ever worked for said, "Phyllis, you smile too much. You're too nice." What he meant was—more hostility. Give it a punch! But I had been working for so many years to get rid of all my hostility and anger and become a good person, that I couldn't take that as simply direction in an art form. I had been reading self-help books for years trying not to hate anybody. Now I understand. It's mock hostility. Now I get more and more and more hostile. It's an art form. But if it's real, forget it!

To disguise anger, the comic must set up a "play frame"—the understanding that nothing that's said and done is meant to be taken seriously. Diller establishes the play frame by her shiny, clownlike costume, her exaggerated remarks, and her cast of imaginary odd characters.

Foremost among them is a husband named "Fang." The repellent wife has long been a stock in trade for male comics. Henny Youngman begs his audience to "Take my wife...please." Using "Fang" as a target, Diller simply reverses roles. Other female comics have also referred to their husbands onstage. But unlike Joan Rivers' Edgar and Totie Fields' Georgie, "Fang" is a comic invention. Diller vigorously denies any resemblance between "Fang" and her two real husbands—Sherwood Diller, to whom she remained married for twenty-five years, and Warde Donovan, whom she divorced in 1975 after ten years of marriage. Diller speaks kindly of both husbands, and channels any anti-husband sentiments into the vituperation that she pours on Fang.

Diller also speaks of her real mother with affection: "My mother was the greatest influence on my life," says Diller. "She taught me Shakespeare, the Proverbs, Benjamin Franklin, and how to apply them to my life. I have molded my life on my mother—my humor, zest, positive outlook, energy, and ability to make fun of myself rather than bad-mouthing others." By contrast, the mother in Diller's stage act is a senile, doddering fool:

> Let me put it this way—she's around the bend. Oh my god! You look in her eyes and you know nobody's driving!

> She's perfectly happy. Sits in the kitchen—kills flies with a hammer. Listens to her records every day of her life. Doesn't play them. Just holds them up to her ear.

Whatever familial resentments Diller might have, her stage relatives are caricatured beyond recognition. One character that the comic does claim to have based on life is an immaculate neighbor, "Mrs. Clean."

> I hate that broad! I call her "Mrs. Clean." I hate her guts! Today I sent her a get sick card.

> If there's anything at all to reincarnation, that bitch will come back as a Brillo pad.

If Mrs. Clean is Diller's successful rival as a homemaker, Fang's mother usurps her very home—coming for a visit (uninvited by Diller) and wreaking destruction.

> We still have a souvenir from her last visit. A Persian throw rug. She sat on the cat.

> How can I describe her? Jello with a belt.

> She sat in our hammock and uprooted two trees.

And, in a paroxysm of comedic rage:

> I'd like to slit her girdle open and watch her spread to death!

The fat mother-in-law works for Diller the way Elizabeth Taylor used to work for Joan Rivers. After noting their own lack of appeal, the comics pour their comic venom onto the real sexual pariah—a fat woman. Mother-in-law jokes have been around for thousands of years—usually told by men. Diller trades on that stock figure and zeros in on her obesity. Sexual cattiness is a cliché of bitchy female behavior. Taylor is noted for her success with men, and Diller's mother-in-law is more successful at getting the attention of the one man in Diller's life—her husband. Focusing on their fatness, Diller and Rivers comedically demolish their rivals.

Obesity is also a sign of self-indulgence. Food-rich, fashion-thin America tempts the palate and torments the weak. Cookbooks and diet books sit cheek by jowl on the bookstore shelf. Women's magazines feature four-color spreads of fudge cake…along with diets and diagrams of sit-ups to flatten the abdominals. The comic, like other women in the audience, is tempted. But she cautions us against giving in—the wages of sin are fat. While we're struggling with our own temptations, we can laugh at the chubbettes.

What about the fashionably thin? If fat women overindulge in food, pretty ones overindulge in sex. The real Diller is an only child. In her act, she concocts a gorgeous, trampy sexpot of a sister.

> By the time she was eighteen she had sown enough wild oats to make a grain deal with Russia.

> She's been in more motel rooms than the Gideon Bible.

> She was the original meter maid—all you have to do is meet her—you got her made!

Diller's sister is like River's sexy girlfriend—Heidi Abramowitz. And both comics tell similar jokes about celebrity versions of the dumb, sexy, sister. Diller herself plays the smart, ugly sister in her stand-up act and sometimes in the theatre. In *Wonderful Town,* the musical version of *My Sister Eileen,* Diller played "Ruth," the clever writer who can't get a man while her sister "Eileen" gets every man in sight. Diller's on-stage ugliness is, of course, exaggerated, but it may accurately reflect the feelings of rivalry of many normal-looking women. As Diller says, "It happens in families all the time, especially where there's two girls."

"Ruth" and "Eileen" each has her own area of competence. Ruth is intelligent, educated, talented, and witty. She is, however, singularly inept at attracting men. As she wryly notes, "Since I've been in New York, I only met one man, and he said, 'Why the hell don't you look where you're going?' Maybe it's just as well. Every time I meet a man, I gum it up." "Eileen," her pretty, younger sister, is less intelligent, educated, and talented, but more adept at playing the feminine role that appeals to men.

Like "Ruth," Diller is clever and accomplished. She is also socially poised, wealthy, and fashionable. While no beauty, she is certainly attractive and has had numerous boyfriends and two husbands. Why then, does she present herself in her act as a sexually repellent harridan, without taste, talent, education, or wealth? Part of the reason may come from the fact that Diller, who charted her career for mass acceptance, early recognized the audience's need to feel comfortable with a woman in what is generally a masculine profession—stand up comedy.

At the time of Phyllis Diller's entry into the profession in the mid-fifties, female comics were practically non-existent. Diller had to wrestle with wanting to be both a feminine woman and a professional comic.

> Comedy is aggressive. That's why men used to hate women comics. That's why there weren't any. They wouldn't let 'em live! Women are not supposed to be bright—and there's no such thing as a dumb comic. Joan Rivers is Phi Beta Kappa. They're not supposed to do anything aggressive. They're supposed to stay in their place, take care of the kids, and not intrude in men's realms. I became aware of this because they'd say, "Ordinarily I don't like female comics, but..." They were trying to tell me I was okay—possibly because I think I never lose my femininity. I may be hostile and aggressive, but I am still feminine. It's a spiritual thing. They feel it. Some women lose their femininity when they start to do comedy. They copy male comics.

To Diller, copying male comics means using obscene language and graphic sexual descriptions—often tinged with hostility.

> Let's start talking about Richard Pryor, Eddie Murphy, Buddy Hackett. Their language would be totally unacceptable from a woman. That doesn't bother me a bit. I don't want to talk like that. When I hear a black male doing that, it doesn't offend me because I feel that's their native tongue. It's not my native tongue. It would be as if I tried to do my act in French. I've known a couple of male comics who onstage are talking about the female vagina, and they're looking for disease. Right now, it makes me ill to even talk about it. But a man gets by with it, gets paid big money. There are people who laugh their heads off at that. Can you picture me talking about the male organ?

Today's female comics are often sexually bolder than Diller, but rarely as raw as an Eddie Murphy or Andrew Dice Clay. The reasons are a mixture of nature and nurture. Males are generally more aggressive by nature; and they are given more societal permission to act out their aggression and sexuality. When women tell aggressively dirty jokes, particularly in mixed company, they are often perceived as unfeminine and usurping the male role.

Diller's own jokes are often based on sexual or aggressive impulses. Her jokes attack her own failure to fit into the role of the desirable female or "Fang's" inability to perform as a husband. But her language is clean. For all her oddity, she is a lady—an act for family audiences—clever, slightly racy, but inoffensive. Diller's appearance underscores her innocence. Her outsized, shiny costume, and long cigarette holder (complete with wooden cigarette) make her look like a toy—or a child playing dress-up. The whole effect is theatrical, deliberately artificial.

Unlike Rivers, Don Rickles, or Pudgie, a female comic whose act consists of taking semi-realistic pot shots at the audience, Diller never gets that close. "I'm really a proscenium act." she says. "It's structured—like playing the piano."

Her audience enjoys her technical virtuosity the way basketball fans appreciate a stunning rim shot and cheers her best jokes with "Go Phyllis!" And Diller learned how to work the crowd.

> When I was first starting out, Stan Freeberg came backstage and told me, "If there's a line that you love, and you do it three times, and it doesn't make it, toss it." So now, if they don't get a line, no matter how much I adore it, it's out.

The result of Diller's craftswomanlike attitude is a rapid-fire series of one-liners—one topping another.

> I get twelve laughs a minute because I edit to the bone. To play to ten thousand people, your act has to be structured for that kind of delivery.

To arrive at that structure, Miss Diller writes about seventy percent of her own material. She acquires the rest from outside writers, tailoring jokes to suit her act.

> A comic is responsible for her own material. That's the basic difference between me and a comedienne or a comic actress. Plus, I work alone, where a comedienne or comic actress works ensemble, and usually the material is written for them—like a movie or a sitcom.

To accumulate material for her stand-up act, Diller takes notes from life, sifting through daily experience for nuggets of potentially funny ideas and refining them into jokes.

> It's something you work on constantly. You don't sit down and write— at least I don't. Professional comedy writers sit down and write in a

room with a typewriter. I mark down ideas, and they germinate. Sometimes I will get an idea that won't get into the show for five years. It might take that long for the idea to really jell or to figure out how to use it in the act.

Aside from her costume and frightwig, Diller's act is not primarily visual. She does no slapstick, little mugging, and conceives her routines mainly in terms of language.

> Every word is timed and choreographed. There are times when I use a grammatical error—of course, on purpose—and the joke word is the last word in the payoff. That last word preferably should end in an explosive consonant. For example, "He bought a zebra and named it 'Spot!'" Or: "She told me to stuff my bra with kleenex, I wish she woulda told me to take them outa the box!" These are the kinds of words you want at the end of your payoff.

Diller's comedy style—a machine gun delivery of jokes—is punctuated by her own raucous guffaw. She sets up the joke in a sentence or two, builds rhythmically, climaxes in a staccato explosion of sound—the joke word, and locks it in with her own laugh.

Her emphasis on the aural aspect of comedy comes out of extensive musical training. She is a graduate of the Sherwood Music School in Chicago and plays concert piano and harpsichord. In the last few years, she has given up performing musically because her schedule can no longer accommodate the demands of daily practice or the logistical difficulties of making sure that every hotel room on the road is equipped with a grand piano. But early in her career, her act was mostly music—playing and singing song parodies.

She shifted to a spoken act because "talking gets you more laughs than singing. I got so I loved to hear the laughs, and I evolved."

Even without the song parodies, Diller is acutely aware of the correlation between music and comedy. She creates a pattern of repeating sounds and verbal structures; the punchline abruptly breaks the pattern, which aurally cues the laugh.

> I did a routine about sukiyaki, where I said, "They cook it on the floor, you eat it on the floor, I stepped in it."

What if Diller had said:

> They cook it on the floor, then you have dinner on the floor; and as for me, I didn't look where I was going, so I couldn't help stepping in it.

The sense is the same, but without the comic rhythm, it's just not funny. As Diller notes:

Comedy is listening—the ear, rhythm, and timing. Also, there is a list of real musicians who are comics that is incredible. We'll start with Victor Borge: piano; Phil Silvers: clarinet; Woody Allen: clarinet; Imogene Coca: trombone; Phyllis Diller: piano; Jimmy Durante: piano; Danny Kaye: conducting; Jerry Lewis: conducting; Sid Caesar was a concert saxophonist. He made his total living from saxophone, one of the best; Johnny Carson: drummer; Charley Kallis: drummer; Morey Amsterdam: cello (his father was first violinist for the San Francisco symphony); Henny Youngman: violin. The list is endless! And even the ones who weren't musicians, I think coulda been or woulda been. Maybe when they were young they just didn't have the instrument. Bob Hope sings like an angel, dances...He was originally a hoofer.

Like the performance of a virtuoso musician, comedic timing is individualistic and intuitive.

It's knowing it, feeling it. Everyone has their own rhythm. Look at Joan Rivers: "Can we talk?" She's got her own rhythm. I have my rhythm. A working ensemble is different. Other people can get in your way. They can step on your laugh. They can step on your line. A comic is used to working alone, he's totally in control of everything. Another actor doesn't feel that at all. A comic feels it, knows it. It is so precise! If you boggle a word, if you mess up one syllable—forget the laugh.

Ideally, this precision of sound builds toward the punch line, which, like a hair trigger, sets off the laugh.

The key word is the joke word. Preferably, it should be an explosive consonant and a one syllable word. You remember The Sunshine Boys, Neil Simon's play about two comics who work together? The whole thing was one guy hated the other guy who kept spitting on him because he had all these explosive words.

The major influence on Diller's comedic style is Bob Hope, whose stand-up act is also built around precision firing a series of gags. Hope first saw her when she was just starting out in small clubs. Her act was bombing, and on discovering that Hope was in the audience, she tried to sneak out the back way. He caught up with her and encouraged her to keep on trying. Today, a large oil painting of the famous comic decorates her Hollywood mansion in the "Bob Hope Salon." Diller credits Hope as being her inspiration and mentor: "We are extremely similar. Early in my career, when I would hear myself, I would hear the same cadence."

While this is certainly true in the sense that both comics rely on carefully honed one-liners, Hope's cool, wise-guy style typically depends on snapping the punchline, then either waiting nonchalantly for the laugh or covering with filler words before speeding on to the next joke. The filler words mean nothing in themselves—Hope might conclude a joke by musing "And I wanna tell you..." He sets up the laugh so that it seems to fall "accidentally" in the middle of his general musing. Feigning indifference, Hope dares his audience to be as slick as he is in order to catch the jokes.

Diller's style is more punched-up. Where Hope plays it cool, she demands the laugh. She hits the joke home then stares at the audience, often jump-starting the laugh with her own raucous "Ah-ha-ha-ha!" Another difference between the two comics is their hand gestures. Hope usually stands with his arms at his sides and his hands either in his pockets or clasped in front or behind him. Diller commands the audience by raising one arm.

> The reason for my cigarette holder is to portray a certain type of woman, plus it gives me an excuse to hold up one hand. It is an attention getter. When you flag a train, you raise your hand. When you get attention from the teacher to leave the room, you raise your hand. Over the years I have found very descriptive uses for the cigarette holder. It projects and is continually used for hostility moves and punctuation marks. These gestures I use are natural for me.

Diller relies less heavily than Hope on topical humor. His act, depending as it does on the latest headlines, requires a large staff of writers to supply an up-to-date series of jokes. (The jokes always reflect Hope's basic persona, but their specific content must be constantly freshened.) Diller sometimes brings in topical references, but the core of her act is her dismal home life. Each comic refines that raw material, bending reality into absurd juxtapositions and exaggerations. "I used to work even more visually," says Diller. "My original material—which I wrote every word—was much more imaginative and less commercial."

One of the funniest bits from Diller's early act is an extended story about a cheese. The story projects a surreal film in the theatre of the mind. As her words create the images, her rasping voice and cackling laughter create a rhythmic soundtrack.

> A friend told me the longer you keep Romano cheese, the better it gets. So now, I kept it three years. And this thing turned mean. Now and then I'd open the refrigerator door and throw it some food. I'd have to walk it now and then. And then it grew this one leg. And it's got this ugly fuzz all over it. And the dogs won't run with it. The other day it raped a tulip!

The friend's advice about the virtues of long-lasting cheese sounds reasonable. Diller's response—keeping the cheese for three years—is borderline plausible, given her character as a domestic incompetent. Next, she makes an imaginative leap—the cheese is alive and "turns mean." Diller copes by feeding and walking the cheese. The doglike cheese grows one leg, is covered with fuzz, and becomes so ugly that the other dogs won't run with it. The images are ludicrous, and depend on the audience's ability to quickly visualize what's happening. She concludes with a non-sequitur: the cheese rapes a tulip. (Note the explosive endings of "raped" and "tulip!" The joke would not be as funny if the cheese had, say, mugged a rose.)

The cheese story is a verbal fantasy. Wild, improbable things are described—but Diller is physically restrained. Says Diller: "I can't do physical slapstick. I wish I could. One of my main problems is when a writer has written in physical things for me to do that I find it impossible to carry off. I am physically delicate to the point of being fragile."

Physical comediennes like Lucille Ball don't concoct elaborate verbal fantasies—they act them out. One of the *I Love Lucy* episodes also featured a somewhat surrealistic cheese. Lucy Ricardo wants to bring a cheese on a plane without paying for the extra weight. So she wraps the cheese in a blanket and treats it like a baby. When a fellow passenger with a real baby sits next to her, Lucy gives the cheese a bottle, and burps it. When the passenger asks the baby's name, Lucy gulps, "Cheddar-uh-Chester!" Left alone, Lucy treats the object like a cheese; the shocked passenger accuses her of child abuse. Finally, to get rid of the cheese/baby, Lucy cuts it into pieces and stuffs it into the horn section of Ricky's orchestra.

Like Diller's material, the Lucy sketch begins with a common situation—saving money on a baggage charge—and extrapolates into absurdity. Since Lucy's fantasy is acted out in the context of a quasi-realistic situation comedy, she must play within the bounds of reality. Her cheese cannot grow a leg or rape a tulip. It can only be treated inappropriately. The humor comes from the tension between the realistic situation and Lucy's exaggerated behavior. But where Lucy's audience can easily see what is happening, Diller depends on her audience's willingness to visualize what she describes verbally.

To gain the mass acceptance she sought, Diller all but abandoned this sort of extended fantasy, which is imaginatively demanding of an audience. "It's not commercial," says the comic, "I would work to total silence in this (gambling hotel) room. You realize that it took me years to be able to work a room this size."

Diller's early act was, in fact, quite cerebral, and her audience was limited. She parodied German lieder, operas, and progressive education.

When I first started out, my main supporters were gay. These chic, small discovery clubs in the old days always had a gay bar. The next group I got, from television, was women. Then came men and children. My goal was to get everyone from three to a hundred and three. Now kids know me, and college students. I can work anything. When you have a goal in your head, it programs you. Things fall into place for what you want.

What helped Diller reach her goal was a self-induced course in strenuous self-improvement. "Life," she says, "is a do-it-yourself kit." At thirty-seven, she was poor, homely, disorganized, and lacking in self-confidence. Stand-up comedy, an outrageous career choice for a woman in the 1950's, demands that the performer, without benefit of music, ensemble, or script, take charge of a room. It provides instant feedback—Diller's twelve laughs a minute. And it is, among other things, an exercise in conquering fear.

I used to be afraid of everything. I was brought up on fear. I was the most shy child. On into my thirties I was afraid of everything. I shook, I was so afraid. Afraid of authority, afraid of bridges, afraid of airplanes. But that book *The Magic of Believing* just turned me around. I read it for two years, and as I read it, I absorbed it. It's a whole system of thought. It teaches you how to deal with everyday life in a psychic way. When I read the book, I was scattered—I was writing, I was painting, I had a job, I had all those kids. Then, I focused and decided, "I'm going to be a comic."

Like any performer, Diller uses her own fears, feelings, life, and appearance as the raw material out of which to construct her act. Even from an early age, one source of insecurity must have been her looks. Diller ruefully remembers: "When I was twelve, I was teased a lot. One day, I took a long look in the mirror and said, "Honey, you'd better settle for inner beauty. I still wish I'd had a choice."

It is a truism that comics need the reassurance of laughter to compensate for insecure childhoods. Diller herself remarks: "The fear of abandonment and actual abandonment have created comics." But despite the insecurities that plagued her youth, right through her thirties, Diller now claims to be at peace: "I have no trouble sleeping. I'm very happy, and I'm never ill."

Some critics have faulted Diller for the artificiality of her act and for the fact that she does little experimentation. None of this fazes

Diller. She considers herself to be primarily a craftswoman and professional. She has discovered a satisfying format that has brought her the mass acceptance and wealth that have always been her goal. Her determination to become a famous stand-up comic and the precision-crafted format of her act echo the pattern of her life: the disciplined piano practice; the pragmatism necessitated by providing for five children; the taste for performing despite a lack of glamour; the desire for personal elegance and beauty that could be achieved only by an expensive wardrobe and plastic surgery; the need to vent hostility coupled with a strong taboo (encouraged by self-improvement books) against really hurting anyone; the wild imagination encapsuled in joke rhythms; and the decision to play a preposterous character with inner conviction.

Diller's onstage character grows out of a calculated balance of power. Her persona, who lacks traditional female power (sex appeal and domestic competence), becomes her vehicle for taking power in a traditionally male profession—stand-up comedy. The comedic actress enacts a role and recites dialogue created by someone else; her character may be dim-witted and unintentionally funny. But Diller performs her own material, and is consciously, willfully clever. She captures the attention of the audience and singlehandedly dominates the proceedings. As a stand-up comic, Diller enters a traditionally male bastion of dominance, awareness, and aggression.

Both her subject matter—sex appeal and domestic competence—and the manner in which she handles it—self-deprecation—are Diller's comedic take on the stereotypical 1950's woman. Some have criticized Diller's comedic style as formulaic, artificial, even anti-feminist. But the fact that she has established and maintained her success for over forty years indicates her comedic creativity, the underlying attractiveness of her personality, and a high degree of perseverance and purpose.

"I'm a believer," says Miss Diller, gazing with sincerity past the theatrically long, fake eyelashes she wears in her act. "Anybody can rise above almost anything—if they believe strongly enough. And I am a believer."

Sources

Diller, Phyllis, personal interview held in her suite at the Tropicana Hotel, in Atlantic City, New Jersey, November 7, 1984.

Diller, Phyllis, comedy act, performed at the Tropicana Hotel, November, 1984.

Engel, Lehman, *Their Words Are Music, Wonderful Town*, by Betty Comden and Adolph Green, (New York: Crown Publishers) p.135.

I Love Lucy, "Return Home From Europe," #1050/153, May 14, 1956.

Parish, James Robert, reprint of his interview with Phyllis Diller, which took place during a seminar held at the American Film Institute, October 18, 1977

Stevenson, Ray, "Inside Phyllis Diller," *Redbook*, August, 1978.

Carol Burnett

Carol Burnett, totally exhausted and outfitted in a nightie that looks like the costume of a medieval clown, crawls into bed. Creeping backwards under the covers, she discovers that her foot is dangling twenty mattresses up in space—and she, the royal heroine of a musical version of *The Princess and the Pea* may be in for some foul play. Making the best of what her befogged brain suspects is an odd situation, she lies down. Abruptly, she bellies upward—feeling a lump. She turns over—this time her rear end pops up—again the lump. She crawls around, poking out her tongue in childish concentration and slaps the mattress in brisk punishment. Then she flops down—only to be immediately jerked up again—feet waving in the air and displaying scalloped bloomers. With a malevolent glare, she suffocates the lump with a pillow and curls up to sleep—until the lump twists her into a pretzel of irritation. She sinks back against the headboard, where royal, silken tassels dangle before her crossed eyes. "All right, lump," she squawks, "look out!"

She bounds toward the offending spot, stamps furiously, jumps up and down, and finally falls down in exhaustion, hitting her head on the lump. She lets out a lengthy moan, grabs the tassel, and attempts to lash the lump into submission. At length, she falls to her knees and glares at the audience with madness in her eyes, baring her teeth like a wounded, but undefeated animal. "All right," she declares, "we take it from the top."

Burnett's role as the insomniac princess in *Once Upon a Mattress*, a 1959 off-Broadway musical based on a fairy tale, spotlighted her talents as a comedienne and singer. She was soon asked to be a regular on *The Gary Moore Show* and eventually starred for eleven years on her own comedy/variety program. She went on to perform in films and other television roles and to establish one of the highest Q (popularity ratings) of any female celebrity. Although her work has included a range of dramatic roles, it was as a brilliant slapstick comedienne that she first endeared herself to audiences as both touchingly vulnerable and ecstatically outrageous.

Thirteen years later, Burnett looks far from outrageous as she strides briskly and punctually toward our luncheon date, hand outstretched in greeting and smiling warmly. Her hair is crisply cropped, her pants suit simple and elegant, her figure diet-slim. (Only the color of the outfit—sizzling magenta—hints at wilder qualities beneath the surface.) Off-stage, Burnett possesses an easy, nonflamboyant attractiveness. She looks like neither a glamorous star nor the cartoon ugly she sometimes played in comic sketches. She looks, in fact, entirely normal—with a touch of class.

But then there's the mouth. Reasonable enough in polite conversation and over the scrambled eggs and liver that comprise her menu, that mouth has been known to slide into a rubber grin, segué into a Tarzan mating call and howl up falsetto screams of fury. She seems so average and yet so astounding that the broad mid-section of America who comprise most of her fans came to believe that if Carol Burnett can succeed, anyone can. "I have a lot of people come up to me and say, 'I told my daughter, if you can do it, she can.'" Burnett says, chuckling. "It's a compliment and an insult at the same time." The actress shakes her head. "A lady came up to me once," Burnett's voice filters, flutelike, through an invisible mint julep, "and said, 'I just love ya. You're so common.'" She guffaws. "I've gotten letters that say, 'Dear Carol, I know this sounds crazy, but I really admire you!'"

Burnett's journey from commonness to stardom was a long and perilous one. Born in Texas, she was taken to Los Angeles at the age of seven by her parents, who were in search of employment. Burnett's mother, who wanted to be a journalist, free-lanced for magazines and worked for a time in publicity at Twentieth Century-Fox. The father, who had trouble holding down a steady job, drank from the time he was in high school. After Carol was born and the financial pressure on the family increased, her mother started drinking too. The lack of regular employment often landed the family on welfare, and the lack of money led to more drinking. This in turn led to domestic quarreling, which sometimes erupted into violence. Burnett learned early to dodge the confrontations between her alcoholic parents. She also learned to avoid her mother's fast and sometimes violent hands when she was on the bottle.

The Burnett parents sporadically separated, and during one of their reconciliations, they had another daughter—Carol's sister Chrissie. By the time Carol was a young teenager, both her father and mother were dead.

Carol was mainly raised by her grandmother "Nanny." "She was a rock," says Burnett, "somebody sober who cared." Nanny was a bit odd—her one room apartment was a clutter of peanut butter and jelly jars, old paper bags, and bits of cloth. More importantly, she was stable, sober, and devoted to Carol. Nanny lived in the same building near Hollywood Boulevard. As her own parents became less and less accessible, Carol moved in with her grandmother—sleeping on a Murphy bed that was permanently pulled down from the wall.

Nanny, a devout Christian Scientist, nevertheless managed to be a hypochondriac with eccentric methods of self-cure—including packing newspapers around her waist to hold in her organs. She made daily declarations to Carol of her imminent demise. But despite her self-dramatization as a frail invalid, Nanny was possessed of a robust survival instinct. By the time she died at the age of 82, she had discarded five husbands and was involved with a forty-year-old boyfriend. When she was over 80, she was apparently still attractive. She had a habit of "accidentally" letting her dress slip up over her knees at parties until someone complimented her on her legs. Then she pretended to be embarrassed and pulled the dress down.

Nanny was also an uninhibited low comic. She had a stentorian belch, and she would take out her false teeth and pull her lower lip over her nose—all of which sent Carol and her sister into fits of giggles. Nanny's broad, physical humor eventually surfaced in Burnett's own comedy style. In fact, she modeled one character—the "Little Old Lady"—directly on Nanny.

> I approached it thinking of my grandmother. She used to run her tongue over her false teeth to make sure they'd stay in because they were store bought. She couldn't afford to go to a dentist and have her teeth fixed. Now some people might say, "You're making fun of old people." But I remember my grandmother doing it and it became a character point with me—it gave me something physical to do.

Burnett eventually made her mark in a style comprised of offbeat vocalisms, facial mugging, and slapstick—often violent. Her taste for this kind of material may have come from growing up with Nanny's one-woman show—coupled with her experience as the daughter of alcoholic parents who occasionally staged violent fights. "I was always most comfortable doing physical comedy," says Burnett. "It's a great release—falling down, getting punched, hitting people back— all the screaming roles."

Early in her career, Burnett's physical excesses had her labeled "The Mugger." Says Burnett: "When I started out, it was the era of mugging. I had a great feel for it, and it wasn't until about the sixth year of our show that I realized I could be funny without crossing my eyes. A growing sense of security made me stop mugging and putting down my looks."

Making fun of peculiarities in one's appearance was standard fare for comics. Jimmy Durante made quips about his nose; Jack Benny was comedically vain about his toupee; and Joe E. Brown poked fun at his mouth. Comediennes like Phyllis Diller or Joan Rivers put down their lack of sexual attractiveness—especially their "flat chests."

The fact that comediennes like Carol Burnett emphasized their supposed lack of sex appeal probably reflects women's general worry about their desirability as a function of their looks and the particular importance of beauty to the female performer. Far more than actors and male comics, actresses and comediennes, even female newscasters, are often judged on their attractiveness. When Burnett hosted her own television variety show, audience members would sometimes twit her about her figure.

> Once someone in my television audience asked what my measurements were. I said: "37-24-38—but not necessarily in that order." It got a big laugh, so for a long time after that I would do put down jokes on myself. I wanted to strike first so nobody else would. It's a self-protective measure.

Despite the anti-feminist implications of Burnett's remark, it does illustrate both her rapport with audiences and her quick wit—two key ingredients of her success. The wit depends on a deft fusion of comic techniques: inappropriateness, comic misdirection, foolishness, and surprise. She sets up a model of a beauty contest figure, applies it inappropriately to herself, and misdirects the audience to think that she foolishly believes that she fits the model. Then in a surprise twist, she reveals the truth—that she is the reverse of a beauty queen. "37-24-38" implies a voluptuous figure. By announcing that the numbers are "not necessarily in that order," Burnett abstracts the numbers from their implied sexiness and reveals a funny alternative meaning.

It's unlikely that Burnett painstakingly analyzed the comic potential of the question and methodically constructed her reply according to a blueprint of comic techniques. In fact, she probably seemed spontaneously witty. But the effect of spontaneity is achieved by the mastery of technique, even on an unconscious level. Just as a ballet dancer makes her astonishing leaps and twirls seem effortless (and may not be able to explain the precise muscle techniques behind them); the comic makes a clever retort seem spontaneous (and may not even be able to explain the comic process behind it.) In fact, explaining the joke takes away the surprise that makes it funny.

Burnett's remark also works particularly well because she diffuses social tension. The audience member publicly questions Burnett's sexual attractiveness. Burnett does not directly challenge the implied hostility of his remark. Instead, she makes it funny through comic exaggeration of her defects. She emerges as the manipulator of the situation—while still retaining audience sympathy as a "nice girl" who is not "well-endowed."

Burnett's self-deprecating humor was typical of comediennes of the late 1950s and early 1960s, and it served to soften audience resistance to the notion of an assertively funny woman. Besides being typical of "women's humor," self-deprecation probably came easily to Burnett because of her own family background. As a child, she had to learn to cope with her parents' sometimes violent tempers, especially under the influence of alcohol. Direct confrontation might have been dangerous. Humor was a better survival tactic.

As a child, Burnett learned the technique of the quick comic quip from her parents, who could also be highly amusing.

> My dad was like a Jimmy Stewart—very laid back funny. My mother and I had a lot of laughs together. She had a great sense of humor—caustic, biting, and not very diplomatic. She wasn't always right, but she let you know how she felt about something or somebody, and didn't back down because of what they were.

Despite the laughs, some of that biting sense of humor left scars on her plain daughter.

> My mother was a petite woman with Joan Crawford eyes. I grew to be five feet six, with buckteeth, stringy brown hair, and ninety pounds wringing wet. My mother was a beautiful woman, and she pretty well

drummed it into me that I'd better not try to make it in the looks department. I think that when I went into comedy, I subconsciously decided to hit myself first before anyone else did. I'll put down my figure. I'll put down my face. I'll do the flat-chested jokes. The kind of humor that was acceptable for a woman was being man-crazy and putting yourself down. I wanted to strike first so nobody else would. That was before the feminist movement took hold, and now, I would never do that.

What Carol's mother did encourage was a career in writing, her own original ambition, telling her daughter to "go out and make something of your life. No matter what you look like, you can always write." For a time Carol was the editor of her high school paper. But she always wanted to perform. When she was still a child, she would put on a pretend radio show for her neighbors. Opening the window, she would holler out an entire show featuring herself as both announcer and guest singer. Her greatest thrill came the day a neighbor yelled, "Turn that damn radio off!" Burnett smiles. "It was fantastic! I was always wanting to be heard, yet be invisible."

The "singing spot" on her radio show probably had its seeds in Carol's own relationship with her talented mother. Says Burnett:

I loved it when I could get her to tell stories or sit in the kitchen and play her ukelele. She had a wonderful ear for music. She taught me all kinds of old songs. I'd sing and she'd do the harmony.

Eventually, Burnett was to create variety shows on network television with musically accomplished co-stars such as Julie Andrews, Beverly Sills, Dolly Parton, and Placido Domingo.

Burnett's television specials with Andrews and Sills featured Carol as the less glamorous, less sophisticated, ostensibly less talented woman (much as she must have seen herself in relation to her beautiful mother). Burnett's co-stars were well-trained sopranos, and fit an idealized mode of ladylike femininity. Burnett herself played the part of the all-American girl—ordinary to the point of plainness. Burnett implies that, like most of her audience, she does not belong at Carnegie Hall or the Metropolitan Opera.

Early in the show, her co-stars intimidate Burnett. But by the end, they reveal their admiration for her down-to-earth personality and talent. Buoyed up by their reassurance, Burnett sings some pop songs in a pleasant alto voice. After a certain amount of kidding around—particularly of the pretensions of "high art," Burnett and her co-stars wind up expressing their mutual affection and singing harmoniously as a team.

In the light of Burnett's relationship with her mother, it is interesting to note the comments of the psychologists Seymore and Rhoda
Fisher.

> We believe that some of the techniques comedians develop are an
> attempt to establish a reconciliation with the mother. They become
> very sensitive to moods and learn to kid in a way to protect her. We
> found that the comic uses humor to protect and comfort people. And
> the person he is particularly trying to protect is his mother.

Burnett's television specials can be viewed as a kind of fantasy rec-
onciliation with a mother figure. Like her own mother, her co-stars
are talented, pretty, and feminine; Carol feels awkward and unappealing. She indulges in a bout of comedic naughtiness (just as the
child Carol refused to confine herself to quiet writing and hollered
out "radio shows" to the neighbors). By the end of the show, the star
appreciates and reassures Carol, giving her the support her real
mother, embittered by her own failures, was unable to give. The
move from farcical antagonism to comfort flavors the shows with
humor and warmth.

Burnett's own weekly variety show offered the same mixture of
comedy and sentiment. The show usually consisted of farcical
sketches interwoven with songs and concluded with Burnett's
singing a touching ballad. The mixture of mockery and adulation
with which Burnett treats opera and the concert stage also sets the
tone for her burlesques of famous film and glamour stars—always
popular sketches on her variety show.

Hollywood films were an important formative influence on the
young Carol Burnett. When she was a toddler, her father briefly managed a movie house. Her mother was working and used the movies
as an all-day babysitter. Later, as a pre-teenager, Carol escaped her
home situation by going to eight movies a week. In the darkened
movie theatre, she entered a fantasy world of beautiful actors, gorgeous clothes, and happy endings. Then she would come home and
pretend to be the glamorous stars of the late 1940s and early 50s.
Eventually, Burnett incorporated her childhood games into movie
spoofs on her own television program.

> I've got the costumes, the wigs, and an orchestra. I've grown up and
> I'm still playing the same games. I've been Betty Grable, Joan Craw-
> ford, Bette Davis, Joan Fontaine. Somebody asked me once, 'Answer
> right away. How old do you feel?' I said, 'Eleven.' It popped right out.

I don't think I ever grew beyond eleven. I guess that's when everything was being ground in.

As a teenager, Carol never admitted her own performing ambitions—acting was for the beautiful people in the movies. When she
graduated from Hollywood High School, her mother encouraged her
to go to journalism school. Burnett wanted the University of California at Los Angeles—which had a Theatre Arts program and no journalism major—and told her mother she was interested in the
playwriting course. But her real ambitions lay elsewhere. Her dream
was the immediate acceptance that comes from performing—the
applause and laughter that translate as love.

Burnett did not have the forty-two dollar tuition fee necessary to
enroll in the theatre program. But she did have an intense imagination, and she started visualizing the arrival of the money from some
unknown source. Every morning she would get up and look in her
mailbox across the lobby of her apartment building. One morning
the mailbox had a white envelope with her name on the outside.
Inside was a fifty dollar bill—left by an anonymous donor.

The first semester at UCLA, Burnett had a small comedy role as a
farm girl in a production of Oklahoma. When she said her line,
everyone laughed. It was a magic moment. For the first time, Burnett forgot her looks and felt, finally, at home. After that, Burnett
appeared in other musical comedies produced at UCLA. When she
performed "Adelaide's Lament" in Guys and Dolls, her grandmother
and mother came to see her and were amazed by her talent and the
audience response.

Carol decided on a career in musical comedy, and started visualizing New York. Again, she had no money, but at the party after her
closing performance exam in Theatre Arts, a man offered to lend her
and Don Saroyan, a fellow student, $1,000—if they would pay it back
in five years and never reveal his name.

Once in New York, she did the usual assortment of odd jobs to sur-
vive. She also married Saroyan, a union that was to last four years.
Finally, newly separated from Saroyan and after just missing out on
Richard Rogers' Babes in Arms, she got a phone call. George Abbott
was directing an off-Broadway show called Once Upon a Mattress and
wanted her to audition. According to her own report, Burnett
remembers riding on the subway to the theatre, feeling calmly certain that she would get the part. Back in California, she had visual-
ized that her first break in the New York theatre would be in a play

directed by George Abbott. True to her vision, she was hired to play the female lead.

Like many of the movie spoofs that were to become staples of her television show, *Mattress* was written as a burlesque on the excesses of femininity. Prince Dauntless, thirty-six years old, has never married because his mother, the Queen, devises a trick test to prove that no eligible young woman possesses the ladylike delicacy of a true princess. But when Princess Winifred (Burnett) arrives at court after swimming the moat and blasts out a ditty entitled "I'm Shy," Dauntless is utterly smitten. To defeat the match, the Queen tests Winifred for aristocratic sensitivity. She places a pea beneath twenty mattresses and gives Winifred a sleeping draught. If Winifred sleeps, it will prove she is too insensitive to be truly royal, and unfit to be Dauntless' bride.

Burnett plays Winifred (nicknamed "Fred") as a hyper-energized tomboy, good-natured, unpretentious, affectionate, insecure, loud, and plain. She is possessed of an outraged squawk, a coy squeal, and a throaty growl to indicate how her wedding night will leave her "thoroughly satisfied." She bats girlish eyelashes—a hairbreadth away from tears—and shoves Dauntless aside with truckdriver machismo to demonstrate her desire to lift weights to pass his mother's test. She puckers up for a good night smooch by shifting her lips horizontally toward Dauntless' mouth—then tenderly touches the kiss he plants on her cheek.

In true fairy tale fashion, Burnett does eventually marry the Prince. In a role reversal, Dauntless takes on Winifred's strength and stands up to his domineering mother. Through his love, Winifred at last believes that she is an attractive woman. Burnett's emotional range gives the part of Winifred vulnerability under the farce, and set her course for stardom.

The elements that worked so well for Burnett in *Once Upon a Mattress* were played out in various shadings in her other sketches and songs. In 1957, Burnett became a television regular on *The Gary Moore Show* and appeared on *The Ed Sullivan Show* singing "I Made a Fool of Myself over John Foster Dulles." With the same gusto that made her so eager for marriage that she swam a moat, she sings of her crush on Dulles with cross-eyed, comical conviction. Wearing a fairy tale crown, she bowls over Moore with good-natured lust, teasing him with "all smoke and no fire...?"

Burnett's own romantic life was more satisfactory. Divorced from Saroyan, she met Joe Hamilton, the producer of *The Gary Moore Show*.

Hamilton, the father of eight children, was separated from his wife. Despite gossip, Burnett and Hamilton were married in 1962—a union that was to produce Burnett's three daughters, and lasted until a divorce in 1982.

In 1966 Burnett was given her own show on CBS—an hour long comedy-variety special that was on the air until 1977. She opened *The Carol Burnett Show* with a question/answer session with the audience. Following that came a series of comedy sketches and some songs. Burnett played a variety of characters, joined by her regular ensemble: Harvey Korman, Vicki Lawrence, Tim Conway, and guest stars. This program formed the core of Burnett's public image and comedic characterizations, and became a springboard to other television specials and films.

As a comedienne, Burnett has tremendous energy, physicality, and a willingness to take "unladylike" risks. Swinging doors dump her into potted palms. Leg casts trip her onto trays of cocktails. Giraffe-limbed and rubber-faced, she lampoons Gloria Swanson in "Sunset Boulevard" as a screaming harridan. She tosses back a hyper-fluffed wig as Farrah Fawcett and coughs her way through Ali McGraw's death scene in *Love Story* like a commercial for Vicks Vaporub. As "Starlet O'Hara," she descends the staircase of a burned-out southern mansion in a dress she has whipped up out of old velvet curtains—complete with curtain rods which poke her shoulders out into line-backer proportions.

She plays her own sexuality for laughs. When handsome guest star Lyle Wagoner touches her, she squeaks with glee and almost collapses. In a spoof on ancient Rome, she plays an empress outfitted like Theda Bara, who makes broad advances to a slave (Sid Caesar), who accidentally stabs her and then calls for an orgy. In 1982, Burnett played "Miss Hannigan" in the film Annie. Miss Hannigan, a sex-starved orphanage superintendent, is close to the outrageous characters Burnett played on her television show. "What attracted me to Miss Hannigan was the chance to do something outrageous on film—to really cut loose the way I do in my TV sketches."

Carol Sobieski, the screenwriter for the musical, comments: "Miss Hannigan is sexually very aggressive, which people can take better in comedy than straight drama." Miss Hannigan's sexuality, like that of many of Burnett's sketch characters, ultimately causes her humiliation. In one scene Hannigan/Burnett is in bed responding passionately to a man making love. The camera pulls back to show her kissing the radio broadcasting the man's voice, as giggling orphans peep at her through the window. She screams hysterically "Get away!" ripping the shade as she pulls it down. Just before Hannigan's shame becomes actually painful, Burnett plays it for laughs by swigging gin from a flower vase. Hannigan's costume is the fashion equivalent of her sleazy attempt at romance. She lunges after the orphans slathered in ruffles, with snagged nylons and a crimson crepe skirt pulled tight across her hips and gathered under her belly in a baroque bouquet of draperies topped by a rosette.

> Something physical can give you a whole new attitude. Sometimes I had no idea what I was going to do with a character until I put the costume on. Then the voice developed, and then the psychology.

Even when Burnett's costumes were not as exaggerated as Hannigan's ruffles, her attempts to be chic foreshadowed social humiliation.

> We've done sketches where Harvey (Korman—a regular on Burnett's variety show) and I played a successful married couple, dressed to the nines. In sketch comedy, the better dressed you are when things happen to you, the funnier it is. What can be funny about having trouble sitting down in a pair of slacks in a restaurant? It's much funnier if you're very nicely dressed in a tight, beaded dress, where you can't really move or even cross your legs and you have no idea he was bringing you to this hamburger joint.

Like glamour, domesticity is a feminine virtue that eludes Burnett. One sketch shows Carol trapped in a malignant version of television commercials for household products. She enters her kitchen wearing a rumpled bathrobe ready to do battle with household laundry. She carries a basket of dirty clothes to the washing machine and opens the lid. A muscular male arm brandishing a popular brand of laundry detergent comes out of the washer. When Burnett tries to put the clothes in the machine, they are tossed out. Again she tries to stuff in the clothes—and again they are thrown out. Finally, she approaches the machine and peers inside. The muscular arm comes out, makes a fist, and socks her in the jaw. She falls back on the floor and crouches there—a wounded, enraged, but cunning animal. She creeps up on the machine, stuffs the clothes in, swiftly slams down the lid, and locks it.

As she is staring at the machine with satisfaction, it shudders and begins to grow—up and up until it reaches the ceiling and smashes the plaster. Burnett trots over to a sink full of dishes and opens a window. Dozens of doves fly in, nesting on her hair and shoulders and filling the kitchen with a wild beating of wings and the prospect of vast quantities of guano. Horrified, she beats them back. Then, shaken, Burnett opens the refrigerator. She emerges with a cracker and margarine—as someone shoves a huge crown on her head. She manages to tear the crown off and flings it aside—a look of profound disgust on her face. By now the washing machine has returned to its former size (amid fallen plaster). She approaches it cautiously and snatches out her clothes. She takes the damp clothes off-camera into the backyard. Moments later, the Ajax white knight gallops past the window. We hear a terrible scream. Burnett staggers back into the kitchen—skewered by a lance. Then she dies.

To gauge the savageness of Burnett's comedy, we need only look at the work of her closest predecessor, Lucille Ball as "Lucy Ricardo." Lucy was famous for getting herself into scrapes, complete with props and ridiculous costumes. But no matter how outrageous the situation or her own behavior, Lucy always remained innocent and unharmed. If she made a sexual advance, it was only toward her husband Ricky. If she became more insistent, it was only when masquerading (along with Ethel) as a ridiculous hillbilly, in an attempt to win back her husband's attention. Lucy did not humiliate herself by failing to attract a man or run a household. She might have been bored by domesticity, but she could manage a home and keep her husband's love (partly by amusing him with her zany antics.)

But Burnett's sketches are an absurd theatre of cruelty, with herself as chief victim. It is comedy of the combat zone: Burnett vs. a malevolent universe. Her spoofs of movie stars are failed attempts at glamour by a fundamentally unglamorous, plain woman. Domestic life does not simply bore her, it attacks her. The White Knight doesn't rescue her, he kills her.

What creates the difference in tone between Ball and Burnett? Besides individual differences between the two comediennes, they appeared in different genres: Ball in situation comedy, Burnett in sketch comedy. The main character in a situation comedy tends to be basically likable and invulnerable. The audience roots for the protagonist, doesn't want to see her hurt, and tends to confuse the actress with her role. But in sketch comedy, the actress can play a variety of roles, including unsympathetic characters who wind up (comically) humiliated; and the audience is less likely to confuse the actress with the role. As a sketch performer, Burnett has the freedom to play everything from villain to victim to fool.

However, for her show to succeed, Burnett must still establish herself as its endearing main character. She accomplishes this by appearing as her good-natured self in her opening question/answer session. In contrast to the farcical sketches, the opening is unrehearsed and "real." Burnett seems almost amateurish—only a step removed from the average audience member.

> When we first started doing the question and answer session with audience, I was frightened. But we decided to take a chance and put it on the air. The questions were wonderful—some of them were so bad even our writers couldn't come up with them and people saw there was truth in it. We'd leave in some dumb answers on my part and times when I was stumped. I don't really look like I know what I'm doing up there.

What audiences respond to when Carol appears as herself is a sense of her "niceness." She is like them—only funnier and nicer. It is therefore, all the more curious that the sketch character most closely identified with Burnett—her personal favorite and the one that comes nearest to reflecting the situation of the average housewife—is Eunice. Eunice is many things—loud, mean-spirited, self-deluded, pathetic, and sometimes drunk. One thing she is not is nice.

Eunice was first developed as a character in a sketch created and performed by writers Dick Clair and Jenna McMahon in the 1960's. Clair and McMahon went on talk shows with a routine about an actor who won an Academy Award and came home to visit his vituperative sister Eunice (played by McMahon) The family ignored him and talked about their dog. (When Merv Griffin played the actor, he picked up McMahon's baby and plaintively adlibbed "I just won the Academy Award.")

When Clair and McMahon revised the material as a sketch for Burnett, they made the brother a writer and added a mother. In one draft, Carol was the mother and Vicki Lawrence played Eunice. Finally, Lawrence was made the mother. McMahon says, "Vicki was astonishing in the role. It was as if she was possessed. She started doing it in her twenties and she never wore any make-up—just that wig and glasses." "We wrote them as mid-Western characters," says Clair. "Jenna's mother is from Kansas City, and we based Mama on her. We expected them to play it straight, but at the run-through, Carol picked up a fan and drawled 'Ooowee! Is it hot!' I thought it was a new character. But every other line was the same, and it was hilarious—and heartbreaking. We wrote Eunice as a thoughtless woman, but Carol put vulnerability into it."

Clair and McMahon, of course, did most of the writing, but Burnett contributed special touches—often based on her own life.

> There's the time Mama gives Eunice the beer. This is after she's already
> called her names for drinking and told her to stop. I felt it was impor-
> tant to put that in because it happened with my grandmother and
> mother once. My mother had been on the wagon for a few weeks when
> my grandmother offered her a drink. It's a common thing in families
> when the alcoholic tries to quit, the other person finds they're left with-
> out a job. I based Eunice on my mother, even though Eunice doesn't look
> like her. My mother was very beautiful, but she felt like a failure, and
> as she got older she tried to find solace in drinking—as Eunice starts to
> do. I remember my mother saying, "If only this or that hadn't hap-
> pened, I could have been something." She made excuses like she couldn't
> leave me. It was the ultimate cop-out of giving up too soon. She was
> bright...Maybe things were stacked against her...I don't know.

As Eunice, Burnett's body finds a slapstick equivalent for the rag-
ing disappointment of her talented, frustrated mother. The eyes pop
with outrage. The voice pole-vaults the registers. The Adam's apple
heaves as she gulps down yet another insult. The arm is flung
upward on a tidal wave of determination—only to sink beneath an
undertow of despair.

When Eunice takes a stab at glamour, she does it with a butter
knife—and drops it on her foot. Her skinny neck is accentuated by a
bodice made of floral chiffon; her mousy brown hair is lacquered into
beauty parlor precision; she attends a funeral wearing a filmy black
dress—and white shoes.

> I wanted to do Eunice with a Texas accent, but I really got into her
> when I saw what Bob Mackie (the costume designer) had me in—the
> wig that looked like she got a permanent every month, the old print
> dress, the taste in shoes.

Eunice was designed as a broadly comic sketch character. But
when Burnett performed the role in a ninety-minute special, the farce
slipped into pathos and a moment of real truth about the hopeless-
ness of Eunice's life.

Eunice is the most memorable and complex of the characters Burnett created as part of her eleven-year stint as host of her own com-
edy/variety show. In both writing and performance, Eunice and her
husband Ed (Harvey Korman) and Mama (Vicki Lawrence) have a
substance that extends beyond their origin as sketch characters. The
"Eunice" sketches became a regular feature, almost a mini-situation
comedy within a variety show. In fact, Vicki Lawrence, who played
Mama, was later able to star in a spin-off sitcom version of the
"Eunice" episodes called Mama's Family.

Burnett's other sketch characters did not evolve with the same depth or appear as regularly. They range from a dumb but buxom secretary to a wistful charlady to a sex-starved Roman empress to scores of movie stars. The roles vary enormously, but beneath differences of costume and character, there are common themes. To find some sort of consistency among Burnett's sketch roles, let's start with Eunice, her signature role.

Eunice's comic mixture of pathos, rage, fantasy, and desperately inept femininity are at the core of many of her other sketches, especially her numerous spoofs on movie stars. Some of these parodies include Gloria Swanson's aging silent movie star in *Sunset Boulevard;* Vivienne Leigh's vivacious Southern belle in *Gone with the Wind;* Ali Magraw's romantically doomed co-ed in *Love Story;* and the glamour roles played by Betty Grable, Joan Crawford, Bette Davis, Joan Fontaine, Rita Hayworth etc. in the 1940's "women's pictures," which Burnett saw as as a teenager escaping family problems.

If the movie stars are models of feminine glamour, Eunice is the plain woman who tries to mimic them with fake pearls, tacky chiffon, and lacquered pincurls. When Burnett plays movie stars, she mocks not only the notion of glamour but also the possibility of herself ever aspiring to possess it. From the moment she appears in costume, the audience is aware that she does not look as beautiful as the original. There is something comically wrong with the way Burnett looks, and the sketches often take on a kind of pathos and anger under the farce.

Even when Burnett plays a child star, she deals with idealized femininity as a source of pain and humor. One of her early sketches spoofs Shirley Temple, a diminutive darling of 1930's movies—and the role model for little girls when Burnett was a child. Burnett's version—"Shirley Dimple"—is a sticky-sweet little girl, outfitted in a confection of ribbons, ruffles, flounces, banana curls, and bloomers that look ridiculous on Burnett's 5'9" grown-up frame.

It is interesting to compare Burnett's "Shirley Dimple" with Lily Tomlin's "Edith Ann." Both are oversized, truculent little girls. But "Edith Ann" is an all-round kid, tomboyish, naive, and smart-alecky. "Shirley Dimple" is "sugar and spice and everything nice"—an adult notion of cute little-girlishness. In fact, "Dimple" is not particularly childlike at all. As played by Burnett, "Shirley Dimple" is actually an aging, bad-tempered, over-the-hill actress. "Shirley Dimple" is in many ways a younger, sillier version of another of Burnett's sketch characters—the reclusive, self-absorbed, ultimately mad, has-been movie star of *Sunset Boulevard.*

Like the actress, Eunice is forced to face her own aging and the collapse of her dreams of glamour. She turns from such self-knowledge with comic outrage. Burnett notes that when she played Eunice without exaggerating for comic effect, "The result was pure Tennessee Williams." Williams is famous for his portrayal of tragic Southern belles, the most famous being Blanche Dubois, the nymphomaniacal descendant of plantation owners who drifts into mad fantasies of gentleman callers. Blanche's ladylike pretensions give her an air of poetic vulnerability. Eunice, a would-be southern belle trapped in a life of drab domesticity, is seen from a comic perspective and becomes ludicrous.

Many of Burnett's other sketches show her as a housewife and mother. But while the situations are ordinary, they are rife with humiliation, resentment, and slapstick violence. Christmas card notions of the holiday season present a vision of peace on earth and warm family togetherness. Burnett's Christmas sketches are comic minefields of psychic pain. In one sketch, Burnett anticipates an affectionate holiday with her husband. But she soon finds herself insulted. She returns tit for tat and winds up in an argument that culminates in a slapstick fight.

Another sketch is based on Burnett's real experience in raising a teen-age sister while married. She bribes a neighbor's son to take the sister on a walk so she can be alone with her husband, hoping for a romantic evening. But her husband ignores her to read the newspaper. The date turns out poorly (the sister carries her date over a mud puddle and drops him). When the sister retreats into the kitchen, Burnett bets her husband that her sister is crying her eyes out—he says that she is simply stuffing her face. The sister emerges from the kitchen with a huge sandwich, pushing open a swinging door to dump Burnett into a potted palm.

If Lucille Ball plays the American housewife as an adorable clown, then Burnett plays her as an angry victim. Burnett points out the difference between her sensibility and that of Ball:

> Ball's comedy came out of an era that was all fun and nonsense. When I started on The Gary Moore Show, it was the same way—all slapstick and kooky—nothing biting. Then along came Mike Nichols and Elaine May, cerebral satirists who were also terrific comedy actors. I was in the middle of an evolving period of comedy. I hope I changed right along with it. Our comedy could be a little darker because of the times. Then along came Lily Tomlin who was even darker.

Another motif that runs through Burnett's sketches is that of Burnett as the inept sexual aggressor. In a contemporary sketch set in a ski lodge, Burnett plays an accident-prone husband-hunter who has gone skiing in hopes of meeting a man and winds up with a broken arm. Stuck in the ski lodge, she meets a man who broke his leg when she tripped him with her luggage. As she pursues him,she accidentally spills hot rum down his shirt, pierces his hand with a pen, and lands them both on the floor in a heap of new injuries.

The inept sexual pursuer is a traditional comic type played by both men and women. Since the 1960s, films and plays have sometimes featured male heros who are homely, socially clumsy, yet ultimately successful in their romantic ambitions (For example, the bumbling Woody Allen character in *Play It Again, Sam*, wins over pretty Diane Keaton.) But when the female acts as the pursuer, she is shown as unattractive, unfeminine, and unsuccessful. In many of Burnett's sketches, she pursues her male co-stars; the audience laughs at the way she mocks her own unattractiveness; and she rarely gets the guy.

Her supposed lack of femininity leads to other tomboyish behavior. She is famous for her "Tarzan yell"—an ear-blasting version of the macho call of the "King of the Apes." On one of her variety shows, she suddenly bursts into a deep-voiced rendition of a song sung by the male lead in *Carousel:* "I wonder what he'll think of me / I guess he'll call me the old man."

On another show, Burnett performs a duet with the soprano Julie Andrews. Burnett describes Andrews as the quintessential lady. Andrews in turn sings about Burnett's down-to-earth appeal: "You're a little kid at a ball game waving his pennant in the breeze / you're our boys overseas!"

The underlying premise of many of her sketches is that Carol Burnett is an essentially unfeminine, un-beautiful woman who does not fit the idealized feminine image our society assigns to women. Her comedy satirizes that image and plays her failed attempt to fit into it for laughs. Her characters cannot get hold of what seems to be expected of them as women. Confronting their own failure with bruised defiance, they are angry, outrageous, pathetic—and funny.

Conventions of sex role behavior are not the same as actual behavior or feelings. One of Burnett's charms as a performer has been her willingness to expose the insecurities that plague most women. For every woman who feels like a model of lovely femininity and the object of romantic desire, there are probably dozens who feel plain and awkward. And instead of being pursued by glamorous male co-stars, most women know that (however uncomfortably and indirectly) they do their share of pursuing ordinary guys. Paradoxically, it is Burnett's lack of conventional femininity that makes her more like the average woman. Her rebellion against the burden of glamour and feminine stereotypes gives her the common touch that is the key to her funniness and popularity.

The radical questioning of conventional roles was part of the social upheaval that characterized the late 1960s and 1970s. Burnett's comedy/variety program did not reflect the social clashes of the time as directly as, say, the Norman Lear situation comedies of the 1970s, which took their subject matter from contemporary controversies. But Burnett's show, which began in 1966 and lasted through 1977, was also a product of its time, both because it was the most successful comedy/variety show to be hosted by a woman and because of its sensibility.

As Burnett notes, *I Love Lucy* came out of the 1950s, the age of surface conformity. In keeping with its era, *I Love Lucy* projected an image of stable, happy domestic life, spiced with innocent zaniness. (The serious conflicts of the Ball/Arnaz marriage, which ultimately culminated in their divorce, were never permitted to surface.) Burnett's own sketches were rife with conflict and anger between characters and with its star's conflicted attitudes toward women's traditional roles.

After her own comedy variety show closed, Burnett moved into films—often in dramatic roles. In these roles, she expressed a depth and complexity that had been only hinted at in her broader sketch characters. She played Walter Matthau's wife in *Pete 'n Tillie*, a film about a troubled marriage; she followed this with serious roles in Robert Altman's *Health and A Wedding*; and she played a wife who demands emotional honesty, including anger, from her husband Alan Alda in *The Four Seasons* (a role that combined both drama and realistic, domestic comedy). She starred in dramatic specials on television, playing an outraged mother determined to find out the real circumstances of her son's death in *Friendly Fire*; she portrayed a reformed alcoholic who founds a home for women in *Beatrice*; and in *Between Friends* with Elizabeth Taylor, she played a newly divorced, fiftyish woman, who puts together a new life.

This last film, aired on HBO in 1983, began shooting a year earlier, soon after Burnett's divorce from Joe Hamilton. Her three daughters are now adults—including Carrie, who as a teenager fought a highly publicized battle against drugs.

The publicity around Carrie happened about the same time as Burnett's equally public battle against *The National Enquirer*. She sued the publication for libel when they stated that she had been drunk and disorderly in a Washington restaurant and won the case. The libel must have been particularly painful in the light of Burnett's own family history. In a 1983 interview with Barbara Walters, she said: "I have wine with dinner, but no hard liquor. I've read that alcoholism is hereditary, but fortunately, hard liquor makes me ill. I wish everyone was like that."

In 1986 Burnett published *One More Time,* her autobiography. She began co-writing a second book with her daughter Carrie about the process of overcoming drug abuse. Carrie finished her part of the book; but Burnett never concluded hers because she was reluctant to expose certain other personal relationships, especially her divorce from Joe Hamilton. With a perspective gained from time and therapy, she now looks back at her marriage and childhood with insight and compassion, remembering Hamilton's charisma and humor and admitting her own difficulties in relationships as partly stemming from growing up without a strong father figure.

In 1990, Carol returned to television with her own series: *Carol & Company.* The program, a weekly anthology of short plays, mainly funny, but with strong elements of drama and pathos, was a daring format for network programming. Each episode was an independent story, with Carol playing a different character in a new situation, supported by an ensemble cast and guest stars.

The anthology format had not been successfully attempted on television since *The Loretta Young Show,* and never with comedy. But Burnett refused a standard situation comedy format (which she imagined would be a kind of "Granny Goes to College," with herself as a motorcycle-riding grandmother having a romance with her professor while her adult children clucked disapprovingly). Instead, Burnett insisted on stretching her dramatic talents with a variety of roles, including a transsexual woman who goes to her high school reunion—where she had been the male captain of the football team—and faces her high school sweetheart. Like her earlier variety show, Carol & Company was both a popular success and a personal triumph for Burnett, who was able to break new ground as a performer.

Burnett now speaks of her childhood situation with gentle humor, although as a child, she remembers feeling unloved and being terribly angry at her parents. She also seems at peace with her looks. A recent operation to correct her bite had the side effect of giving her more of a chin, about which she giggles: "I'm prettier now."

Burnett's talent and achievement are extraordinary. She is an expressive singer, dancer, comedic and dramatic actress. She was the sole successful female host of a comedy-variety show. (Earlier attempts by Martha Raye and Imogene Coca, among others, had not succeeded.) Burnett took charge of an entire show, spoke directly to her audience, and appeared as a wide variety of characters in the sketches. Like a stand-up comic such as Phyllis Diller, she was obviously in charge. To soften the impact of her power and competence, Burnett appeared at the beginning and end of each show as herself— unsure, unpolished, and overwhelmingly nice.

Many comics ingratiate themselves with an audience by presenting themselves as insecure and get a lot of laughs based on their supposed comic inferiority to the audience. Even more than comic roles, traditional sex roles demand that women be dumber and weaker than men. This expectation was even more rampant in the pre-feminist era when Burnett began her performing career than it is today. As the host of her own long-running, successful show, Burnett was clearly a powerful woman. But like Diller's jokes, Burnett's sketches usually portray her as inept and/or abused, especially in traditional feminine arenas of domesticity and romance (for example, the extended pantomime in which she is attacked by commercial household products and skewered by a White Knight).

This sketch, tailored to display Burnett's gift for broad physical pantomime, is both very funny—and painful. The dichotomy of laughter and pain is, of course, not unique to Burnett. Most comedy is the transformation of some kind of personal pain. The release of that pain, the transformation into humor, reassures us that our troubles are not overwhelming but ultimately laughable. When the performer is honest and vulnerable, even in the midst of the most outrageous slapstick, we experience not only entertainment, but shared humanity and hope. Burnett's comedy is a creative, often brilliant metamorphosis of her own personal history into universal communication. Carol Burnett's gift as a performer has been her ability to use the raw material of her own life to create both empathy and laughter.

Sources

Burnett, Carol, personal interview, conducted at the Polo Lounge in Los Angeles, California, June 22, 1982.

Burnett, Carol interview with Barabara Walters, NBC, May 12, 1983.

Clair, Dick, personal interview conducted at Jenna McMahon's home in Hollywood, California, June 22, 1982.

Dworkin, Susan, "Carol Burnett—Getting On With It," Ms., September 1983, p.43.

Fisher, Seymore and Rhoda, *Pretend the World is Funny and Forever*, (New York: Random House,1981) p.52.

The Gary Moore Show, CBS, June 12, 1957.

Hammerstein II, Oscar and Richard Rogers, "My Boy Bill," *Carousel*, vocal score published by Williamson Music, Inc., 1945.

McMahon, Jenna, personal interview conducted at her home in Hollywood, California, June 22, 1982.

Julie and Carol at Carnegie Hall, CBS June 11, 1962.

Meryman, Richard, "Carol Burnett's Own Story," McCall's, February 19, 1976, p.165.

Once Upon a Mattress, CBS Television, December 12, 1972.

Sobieski, Carol, personal interview held on the film set of *Annie*, June 9, 1982.

Joan Rivers

"Grab and take! Grab and take!" meows the manicured blond, stalking the nightclub stage like a pedigreed cat after a common but delectable mouse. She hunches her narrow shoulders over the microphone and calculates the cost of the a rather ordinary engagement ring in the first row and yowls: "Yes! And bury it with you. If the next bitch wants it, let her dig for it!"

A sharp gasp ruffles the minks and polyesters and explodes in a gust of laughter. Joan Rivers grins into the spotlight and fluffs her hair, whipped into a pale gold meringue by her hairdresser "Mr. Phyllis." The laugh confirms it—the audience is hers—tucked neatly into her raw silk, designer label pocket.

And she is one of them—or so she implies with every jibe at housework, gynecologists, and her own figure problems ("I wear an A cup and take a tuck. Does that make you happy, Long Island!?") When Jackie Onassis, then a national idol, married Aristotle Onassis, she jeered: "I respect Jackie Onassis! Marrying that fat old ass! A few schtups and bang! You walk away with twenty-six big ones!" Rivers wheels abruptly toward a be-minked matron. "What about you? Would you jump into bed with Onassis for twenty-six million dollars?" The embarrassed woman shakes her head and Joan shrugs: "Grow up!"

She turns to a woman in the front row woman and asks her what she does. Upon hearing that the woman is in law school, the comedienne sneers, "*Just* what you need, Become a stewardess or a nurse: they marry rich." Laughing along with her audience, Rivers recovers long enough to croak, "Can we talk!?"—then moves on to her next target: breast feeding, body hair, and female body functions ("So what size Tampax do you wear?") Rivers is the material girl of stand-up comedy, using shock tactics to look under our skirts and expose our feet of clay, and our bunions of greed, envy, and lechery.

If Rivers' act is *Lifestyles of the Rich and Famous* seen through the dirty lens of *The National Enquirer* and etched in comic acid, her own lifestyle is elegant, tasteful, and structured around long days of hard, disciplined work. Her New York duplex is full of eighteenth century antique furniture, damask draperies, a grand piano covered with framed photos of celebrated friends, a dining room with a view of the Central Park skyline, and shelves and shelves of books (Joan is an avid reader.) This gracious, formal home displays two sides of Joan's multi-faceted personality—the grande dame and college professor. "I would love to lecture on the eighteenth century in colleges" she confided to a reporter, "with a make-up man at my side at all times, of course."

She has, of course, other facets, alternating the polished surfaces of a lady with the cutting jibes of a stand-up comic. Joan Rivers is the Queen of Diamonds—real and fake. The costume jewelry she sells on QVC cable shopping network. The real gems she extols in her comedy act. ("Any woman who sleeps with a man without jewelry is a slut and a tramp!") To the onstage Rivers, the most important jewelry is a woman's diamond engagement ring, which is both materially valuable and a token of ultimate feminine achievement—marriage to a man who can provide financial security. When an audience member confides that she is engaged, Rivers counsels:

> If he wants the ring back, you swallow the stone. No man will look through shit for a diamond...

This is the "act," the vulgar "Vegas Face" about whom the offstage Joan Rivers has said, "Even I wouldn't have her for dinner!"

Despite her onstage obsession about marriage, a very strong facet of the off-stage Rivers is her focus on career. Widowed in 1987, Rivers sought solace in stand up comedy, "surviving joke-by-joke." Says Rivers: "My work is my catharsis. It's what saves me." One month after the death of her husband, she started appearing on *Hollywood Squares*. She soon moved onto nightclub stages, reframing her grief into JAP jokes:

My husband left in his will that I should cremate him and then scatter his ashes in Neiman-Marcus. That way he knew he would see me five times a week.

Yet another facet of the real Rivers is her talent as a dramatic actress. Like many comediennes, she originally wanted to perform serious roles. ("But I wasn't pretty enough or pushy enough to make it as an actress.") This ambition was encouraged by her husband Edgar Rosenberg. Ironically, it was not fulfilled until a year after his death when she starred as the bitter, neglected wife in the critically acclaimed Neil Simon play *Broadway Bound*, and later in *Sally Marr...and her Escorts*, a one woman show based on the life of Lenny Bruce's mother, which she co-wrote with Lonny Price and Erin Saunders.

In a second ironical twist, her dream of hosting her own talk show, which was also encouraged by Rosenberg, was also completely realized only after his death. She got her first big break on *The Tonight Show* with Johnny Carson in 1965 and went on to become a popular guest host, regularly filling in for Carson until she left to host her own show for Fox Television, which was produced by Rosenberg. But this show, patterned after *The Tonight Show* and placed in the same time slot, was fraught with conflict and enjoyed only a brief run before it was taken off the air. It wasn't until a few years later, that the recently widowed Rivers confounded her critics and scored a major hit with her daytime program *The Joan Rivers Show*. The show, which premiered in 1989, attracted huge audiences; and Joan's own blend of warmth, gossip, silliness, comic repartee, and incisive questions garnered her an Emmy as best talk-show host of 1990.

At the awards ceremony, dressed in a chic white Ferré suit, she delivered a tearful, stinging acceptance speech. She began by thanking her syndicator Tribune Entertainment: "They taught me what it's like to work with honest, decent people"—taking a veiled swipe at Fox, who had canceled her previous show and fired both herself and husband/producer Edgar Rosenberg, who had guided her career for twenty-two years. Shortly after the show was taken off the air, Rosenberg, who suffered from a heart condition, had a heart attack and barely survived a bypass operation. On returning home from the hospital, he sank into depression and committed suicide shortly thereafter.

Dissolving in tears, Rivers concluded her speech by saying "...my husband had a breakdown, and it's so sad that he's not here, because it was my husband Edgar who said, 'You can turn things around.' And except for one terrible moment in a hotel room in Philadelphia when he forgot that…This is really for him. Because he was with me from the beginning. And I'm so sorry that he's not here today."

The last, but not least facet to Joan's career is her writing. She creates much of her own comedy act (along with editing and rewriting the jokes she buys) and authors books and screenplays. She wrote the screenplay for *The Girl Most Likely To*, a top-rated ABC movie of the week, and *Rabbit Test*, a low-budget theatrical feature that has become a cult favorite. She authored *Jewelry by Joan Rivers* and the very funny *The Life and Hard Times of Heidi Abromowitz*, and *Having a Baby Can Be a Scream*. *Still Talking*, the second volume of Rivers' autobiography, is a continuation of her best-selling first book, *Enter Talking*, which ended in 1965, the year she was discovered on *The Tonight Show*, (where she was introduced as a "girl writer.")

Most of all, she is a survivor: of a childhood and adolescence where she often felt like a fat, ugly misfit; of years of rejection and poverty as a struggling performer; and finally, of her husband's suicide (Her latest book is about bouncing back from personal tragedy). She is also a risk-taker. She overcame her own internal conflicts about abandoning the secure but stifling respectability of her parents' upper-middle class lifestyle to attempt a materially and socially uncertain career in show business. And she took the emotional risk of basing her comedy persona, not on standard jokes, but on her own pain. She confided to a New York YMHA audience in 1991:

> Humor doesn't come out of the good times. It comes out of the anger, pain, and sorrow. Always the anger.

In her own book, *Enter Talking*, she explains:

> The act evolves out of yourself—but not intellectually. It gathers emotionally inside you, in a strange way a by-product of struggle, of a willingness to do anything, try anything, expose yourself to anything, staying in motion because sooner or later those ripples will cause change. This is paying your dues, appearing again and again and again on every sort of stage in front of every kind of audience, until you gradually, gradually acquire technique and a stage identity, which is not you, but has your passion, your hurts, your angers, your particular humor. This is a birth process, and it can be painful.

The raw material for the act is Joan's own life—the fear, anger, and grief transformed into absurd humor, the memories exaggerated and ridiculed until the pressurized balloon of pain is pricked by a punchline and bursts into laughter. To understand the act it is necessary to first understand the woman.

Who is Joan Rivers? Born Joan Molinsky in 1935, she grew up as the daughter of a socially ambitious mother, Beatrice, and a physician father, Dr. Meyer Molinsky. (She took her stage name from an agent named Tony Rivers, who didn't want to send her out on auditions as "Molinsky.") Her mother, Beatrice, was raised in luxury in pre-Soviet Russia as the daughter of a Jewish merchant, Boris and his wife Hannah. When Beatrice's radical brother got into trouble with the government and was threatened with induction into the tsar's army, from which few Jews emerged alive, Hannah fled with her children to America. Newly poor, Beatrice labored in sweatshops. At home, she dined with mended napkins and old-world, formal manners.

At 28, Beatrice, possessed of elitist tastes, limited education, and few eligible suitors, married Meyer Molinsky, who had pulled himself out of a life of grinding poverty to attend medical school. Their union produced two daughters: Joan and Barbara. To support the needs of his growing family and the upwardly mobile lifestyle of his ambitious wife, Dr. Molinsky worked six days a week, from morning till 10 PM. Competing with the free clinic, Meyer began his medical practice by charging masses of poor patients only a dollar for an office visit. His patients adored him, and he loved kidding around with them in an earthy style that his wife despised. But no matter how much he made, it was never enough for Beatrice's minks and the children's private schools; and she in turn suffered from his habit of buying cheap, secondhand goods and taking the family on trips without bringing along enough money to pay the bills. A debt-ridden, workaholic, whose only real appreciation came from his patients, Dr. Molinsky was rarely home or available to his daughters. Joan Rivers has said, "I must have been terribly angry that I did not have a father." (Some psychologists have suggested that the performer's need for audience applause is often a compensation for childhood pain of feeling neglected or abandoned by a parent. Unlike many other performers, Rivers did not come from a broken home, but her longing to connect with an emotionally absent parent may have translated into longing for laughter and applause from an audience. Her anger, the "bitch" persona that puts the punch in her punchlines, may well have started here.)

The crowning achievement of Dr. Molinsky's labors and his wife's upscale taste was their home in the upper-middle class suburb of Larchmont. This house provided a setting for Beatrice's two gems—her marriageable daughters. It provided Joan with a sense of herself as a continuation of her mother's values, as a member of a successful social class…and as an impostor. Inside the home were, all too often, the Molinsky's unpaid bills, fights about money, and tension over Joan's show business ambitions. But even with the tension, living at home provided enough security for Joan to remain there for most of her early adult life.

A temporary exception was her first, brief marriage to a department store heir—ideally eligible by Molinsky standards. When the marriage fell apart, Joan went back to her original dream—a career in show business—even running away from home for a few months to stay in makeshift lodgings with her Italian boyfriend Nick Clemente. This escapade was brought to a dramatic end when Rivers precipitated a fight with Clemente which ended when her parents brought her back forcibly to Larchmont. Her last and vital break was a temporary career move to Chicago as a member of Second City Improvisational troupe. When Rivers returned to the East Coast, she went back to her parents' "dream home." After that, she briefly lived in her own "struggle apartment" in Greenwich Village before meeting successful producer Edgar Rosenberg, whom she married at the age of thirty-one.

Like her mother, Edgar was a socially ambitious, distrustful loner, who loved elegant possessions and a formal life style. Reflecting back, Joan has said, "I was about to marry my mother."

In another context, and an even bolder bit of self-revelation, Rivers has stated, "I adored my mother, perhaps because in so many ways, I am my mother." It seems clear that her mother's social ambition at least partly fueled Joan's drive to succeed—and to become a society insider with all the trappings of fashionable affluence. But it was her father's earthy sense of humor, the ability to kid around with his "fans"—the working class patients who adored him—that gave Rivers' act the "common touch" that lifted her to stardom.

Her father's obsession with work is also reflected in Joan's own hard-driving career. "I was a stranger with my father, a stranger too, with my sister. The only one was my mother, and yet the half of me that makes my living is my father. That is so ironic."

Joan's comedy act incorporates much of this biographical material. Both her obsession with wealth and her edge-of-hysteria delivery comes from old family tensions. As Joan says, there was "always the anger"—at a father who was not emotionally available and at being forced to witness her parents' fights about money. There was the humiliation of being sent to the headmaster's office with tuition checks that could not be cashed for weeks because her family lived beyond its means. There was the shame of feeling like a fat, unattractive child. There was the frustration and resentment for years of struggle and rejection as a performer in no-pay/low-pay clubs—including a squalid strip joint where the audience booed her off the stage.

On stage, Joan looks like a member of a privileged class—the Molinskys of Larchmont. Her wardrobe and jewelry are expensive and stylishly conservative. Her nails are manicured. Her make-up is impeccable; her coiffure is fashionable. Her face and figure have been enhanced by several episodes of well-publicized cosmetic surgery.

And out of that ladylike surface come a series of outrageous, angry, bawdy, funny comments—the act. Some people find her humor vulgar and crude. Rivers responds angrily that she considers herself a clean act—especially as compared with other comics who are far more outrageous—and that she's subject to a double standard. If so, it's one she herself precipitates. You simply don't expect toilet jokes from a woman who dresses like Audrey Hepburn.

Rivers' comedy act is a jolt of contrasts. She is both an insider and an outsider, classy and déclassé—the private school student— whose family cannot pay the bills; the wealthy celebrity—whose act mocks the elite; the elegant lady—who talks about farts and pooping.

At the time she started out, Joan's looks were a radical departure from the style of Phyllis Diller (and from the fat Jewish mama somatype of Sophie Tucker, Totie Fields, and Belle Barth). Women comics in the 1950's were expected to look strange, unappealing, and non-threatening. Diller and Fields provided the unsexy, wisecracking counterpoint to Monroe's gorgeous, dumb sexpot.

But although Joan talks about her "ugliness," she looks elegant. She is an Oscar de la Renta yenta, a fashionable matron who loves to dish the dirt, often from her "favorite" publication: the *National Enquirer.*

> I read the National Enquirer. Don't you read the *Enquirer?*…Who said no?…What do you read when you go to the bathroom? I open up the *Enquirer* —I automatically go mmgh! …It's replacing bran muffins!"

Basing much of her comedy act on celebrity gossip from the *National Enquirer,* which boasts that it has "the largest circulation of any paper in America," was a shrewd career move for Rivers. Just as her father had built a successful medical practice on large-volume, low-priced treatment of the poor and was most comfortable when kidding around with his working-class patients, Joan built a star comedy career on her common touch.

She is fond of quoting newspaper mogul William Randolph Hearst, who built a news empire by targeting the common man:

> If you write for the masses, you eat with the classes. If you write for the classes, you eat with the masses.

Like her audience, she loves gossip. Her television talk show features gossip columnists, and her act is peppered with scorching send-ups of the stars.

> Rock stars are ugly. Barry Manilow? A nose? If he were on hard drugs, he could inhale Peru!

> Mick Jagger has child-bearing lips! He could French kiss a moose!

What really boosted Rivers career was spotting Elizabeth Taylor at her heaviest on the cover of *People* magazine and doing a series of "fat" jokes:

> She puts mayonnaise on an aspirin!

> Her car has a bumper sticker that says "My other car's a refrigerator."

Some critics have called these jokes crass, even cruel. Rivers justifies them on the grounds that: "Celebrities can take it…all us entertainers are fair game." And no matter how much audiences might pretend to disapprove, "they have always dictated with laughter what they want to hear." She insists that she never intentionally hurt anyone, that Delta Burke and Elizabeth Taylor sent word that they did not resent the fat jokes, and that, in fact, her jokes goaded Taylor into losing weight!

Despite her critics, Rivers' success with mass audiences seems to indicate that she taps into a vein of anger at the lucky few who have made it—the resentment of the outsider toward the insider. In fact, Rivers' comic persona is based on the tension between her sense of herself as both an outsider and insider.

This tension is the underlying dynamic of her comedy album *What Becomes a Semi Legend Most?* The title plays on her uncertain status among the truly great who are said to be "legends in their own time." The cover features a photograph of Rivers in mink—a take-off on the advertising campaign which shows a glamorous celebrity draped in a Blackglama coat. Rivers, a "semi-legend" with a mink coat falling seductively off one bare shoulder, isn't quite entitled to the respect accorded a real celebrity insider. She may look like an insider, but like her audience, she remains outside real social acceptance—like a child whose nose is pressed against the window as she looks in at a wonderful party—to which she hasn't been invited.

One of the most elite parties of the last twenty years was the wedding of Prince Charles and Lady Diana. Edgar Rosenberg, Joan's English-Jewish husband, emulated the upper-class tastes of the British Royal family. But the Windsors of Buckingham Palace comprise a WASP inner circle beyond the reach of the Molinskys of Larchmont (although Beatrice's best friend did have an affair with an earlier Prince of Wales).

Rivers' fascination with these royal "insiders" led to her devote an entire hour of her talk show to gossip about their private lives. She also features them on the back cover of her comedy album: a formal wedding portrait of Prince Charles and Diana with the Royal Family and one "wedding guest"—Joan Rivers. Gussied up in a shocking pink cocktail dress and ostrich feather hat, Joan displays her wedding present—a blender topped by a satin bow.

Like her fans, Joan will never fit her foot into the glass slipper and live in the royal palace. But she can invite them to join her on a comic journey of derision at what they envy, resent...and admire.

> The Royal Family? A bunch of Dogs! Go out on the street, call their names: "Queenie, Duke, and Prince." See what shows up!

> Prince Charles? Those stupid ass ears on him! He'll hang glide over the Falkland Islands.

> Queen Elizabeth. Is that a schlep?! Can we talk? If you're rich you should look good. If you own England, Ireland, Scotland, and Canada—shave your legs!

Besides being a royal family portrait, the album photograph is a wedding picture, with Joan as the misfit guest. If Princess Diana is the insider (especially before her marital troubles made tabloid headlines), Joan is the awkward outsider. Rivers certainly had plenty of painful experience with this role. Through most of her twenties, Joan was not only struggling with a frustrating career, she was also an unmarried daughter who served as a bridesmaid at the wedding of many contemporaries.

While twitting celebrities enhanced her career, the original core of Rivers' onstage persona was her portrayal of the unattractive, sassy girl whose desperate mother is pushing her to get married.

> I was twenty-eight when I got married. My mother had a sign: last girl before freeway.

> I was dating a transvestite. My mother said, "Marry him. You'll double your wardrobe!"

With the exception of an early, brief marriage, Joan was single in the fifties and early sixties—before women's liberation, the sexual revolution, and widespread divorce. It was a time of minimal social support or acceptance for an unmarried woman. It was out of those years that she created the core of her act: a wisecracking, single girl who is dying to find a husband.

It was this persona that finally in 1960, brought her to the attention of Bob Shanks, talent coordinator for *The Jack Paar Show*. It seemed as if her big break had come at last, and she went on the air with a line of comedy chatter that was an exaggerated version of her own trials and tribulations. Sitting across from Paar in his talk show format, she confided that her mother was so desperate to marry her off that she painted the kitchen pink because pink was supposed to make girls look good. She even bought a pink stove and refrigerator. But nothing worked—except that three maids ran off with delivery boys. Rivers talked about her survival tactics at temp jobs (including stealing stamps and selling them to friends wholesale) and working in Mafia nightclubs where the cigarette girls sold bullets.

The audience response was enthusiastic, but Paar failed to understand that she was telling jokes disguised as talk show chatter. He believed that she was simply lying. Rivers was never asked back on the show. Disappointed and confused, she retreated from her own strength—comedy based on the pain of her own life—and went back to doing pointless, cutesy revue jokes. Her career stagnated.

The first major turnaround came when she was hired as a member of the Second City improvisation company. in Chicago. The Second City show consisted of a mixture of prepared skits and scenes that were improvised on the spot based on audience suggestions. The experience of improvising in front of an audience was terrifying to Joan, who was used to working off a script or prepared stand-up comic routine. But finally, she began to get the hang of it, and she soon found the improvisation exhilarating—the magical channel to her own creative source.

> ...whatever your partner did, you used it, responded to it, as you would in real life. That is one reason I talk to people in the audience—so I can work off them as a piece of reality, use them to trigger inspirations, make them into my Second City partner....I learned to have supersensitive antennae tuned to the audience and follow the laughter wherever it leads, improvising deeper in spontaneous, lucky premises, building them, honing them, no matter how outrageous.

The feeling of improvisation is also the root of Rivers' famous signature lines: "Can we talk?" "Oh, Grow up!" "Oh, shshsh!" (added after a punchline) and her emphatic "Yes!" All these lines imply an interaction with the audience—her reaction to their groans of disbelief, embarrassed silence, applause, or laughter. Working alone, Rivers makes the audience her improvisation partner and confidant. Some of her funniest lines are ad-libs in response to something that happens with the audience.

One problem with ad-libs is that their effect depends on the audience's delight with the split-second response of the performer to a specific situation. Often, they are as ephemeral as they are brilliant. A second problem is that, even if the ad-lib does have enduring cleverness, it's gone forever, forgotten as soon as it's said. Rivers set out to conquer both problems. Urged by her best friend Treva Silverman, who lent her a Wollensack tape recorder, Rivers began taping each show, replaying the act and re-using the lines that worked. These lines could either be incorporated into the act, or mentally filed away to be used as seemingly spontaneous ad libs whenever a similar situation arose. Since Rivers' act centers around a repertoire of related topics, it is highly likely that a similar situation will come up, at which time, the successful joke can, with minor modifications, be plugged in.

Another signature motif of Rivers is her "spontaneous search" for celebrities in the audience. This motif began as a search for the Queen of England, who was supposedly following Joan around from nightclub to nightclub. The routine got laughs and gradually expanded into a search for other notables such as Nancy Reagan and Dr. Ruth, the 4'7" sex therapist—who might be hiding under the table!

Second City also stressed the imaginative use of props, often pantomimed. To this day, Rivers incorporates a "spontaneous" use of props in her act. In the 1991 Tropworld Christmas show, Rivers walked onto a stage decorated with potted poinsettias in straw baskets. She strode over to the plants, pulled off the straw basket, sets the basket on her head, and announced with cockeyed practicality, "I can wear it to the beach."

Second City also gave Rivers the opportunity to create a scene based on the character of "Rita, a single model." Rita, an urban, ethnic loser with men, was an exaggerated comic version of Joan's own struggles as a single girl, and became the core of her stand-up act. When Joan went back to doing stand-up comedy, Rita surfaced in jokes about her rejection by a college date who was so indifferent to Joan's sexual charms that his hand fell asleep—in the middle of petting!

If Joan/Rita is the outsider, the female failure who can't get a man, the insider is the married woman. Joan's first model for a married woman was her own mother. Rivers' comedy persona speaks for both the pressured single woman and for the parent who is applying the pressure—the comically exaggerated voice of her own mother.

Maternally accusing, she interrogates female audience members:

> Are you married?...How old were you when you got married?...Did you wear white?....Are you a nurse?

Then, abruptly switching to her daughter self, she confesses:

> I wore white....I had a big, black hem on the dress. When the Rabbi said, Do you take this woman? Sixteen guys said "We have."

In another abrupt shift, she sniffs with maternal contempt:

> Any woman who sleeps with a man without jewelry is a slut and a tramp!

The humor of this line is based on its reversal of respectable expectations. According to respectable mores, sleeping with a man for jewelry brands a woman a prostitute—in other words, a slut and a tramp. In a comic reversal, Rivers announces that sleeping with a man for love or pleasure is suspect—only jewelry lends respectability to the act. The audience's laughter acknowledges the germ of truth in her outrageous suggestion that society honors prostitution as long as it wears the veneer of respectability—an engagement ring.

Ironically, before her marriage to Edgar, Joan herself had a few passionate affairs without benefit of jewelry—engagement rings or otherwise. The slut and tramp she is talking about is herself—or at least her youthful, indiscreet self.

When Joan did get married, she had to adapt her persona of the loser single girl to the loser wife and aging matron.

> I have no sex appeal. If my husband did not toss and turn in his sleep, we never would have had the kid.

Now that she is a widow, Rivers jokes about her non-existent love life. From single woman to wife to widow, the core of her comedy persona remains the same—Joan is the sexual loser, the ugly girl whom no man wants.

Like most comedy, Joan's persona came out of personal pain. Joan remembers being an outsider at school, a chubby unattractive child whom schoolmates dubbed a "fat tub of lard" and "fat, fat, water rat."

> They were right—I was fat, so I hated myself even more, seeing myself as this huge thing with knees that could have fed China for a year. I felt as if everything I ate went instantly to my thighs—like a squirrel

storing food in its cheeks—and to this day, no matter how thin I am, that is my image of myself.

This image comes out not only in Joan's comic belittling of her own figure—especially her "fat" thighs but also, moving from victim to aggressor, in her vituperative jokes about female celebrities who are fat or unattractive. In her comedy act, she becomes both the ugly, teased scapegoat and the pretty, catty schoolmates who inflict the teasing.

> Talk about *ugly?* Look at my face! *Fat?* Look at my thighs! I don't make fun if it really hurts people. Elizabeth Taylor and Delta Burke said it didn't matter. Barbra Streisand *is* ugly. Who would you rather sleep with—her or Michelle Pfeiffer?"

To be successful, a comedienne needs to not only play off her own psychology but also to relate to the psychology of the crowd. Rivers knows her audience. She knows that, like herself, they both admire and resent attractive, successful celebrities; and they enjoy seeing the rich and famous as the butt of jokes. What the *National Enquirer* accomplishes with gossip and unflattering photographs, Rivers does with caustic humor.

Rivers also realizes that, to her audience, she herself is part of a celebrated inner circle. She dresses like a star, hobnobs with the famous, and speaks freely about her high income. But if all of this creates admiration and envy, Rivers' self-deprecatory humor evokes empathy and assures them that underneath, she is like them—an outsider who feels like a loser.

> Childhood suffering? Not material suffering. But I was chubby, and we lived beyond our means. I was loved, but if I say I wasn't wanted, it's okay that I'm onstage in $200 shoes.

> Talking about my unattractiveness relaxes the audience. There's a grain of truth in it, but I don't take it completely seriously. It's what women do. We put ourselves down to put each other at ease.

Male comics also use self-deprecation. Rodney Dangerfield, Rivers' contemporary, friend, and sometime collaborator, built a career on variations of his trademark line "I don't get no respect."

Woody Allen is also known for his self-deprecating "poor schnook" character. His portrayal of a shy, intellectual bumbler has endeared him to audiences on stage and film. Allen was often booked at the same small Village clubs as Rivers, and in fact, for a time, they even had the same manager. They were both urban, Jewish, clever, and presented themselves as comical sexual losers. Allen became famous before Rivers, and to some extent, his success paved the way for hers. Joan comments:

> When I first came out, I was called female Woody Allen. The difference is he talks about Kafka, and I talk about the *National Enquirer*. I've read Kafka, and I'm bored with it. Besides, I wanted to reach a broad audience.

Is Rivers just another variation on an asexual, "loser" comic persona? Is the comedy of men and women interchangeable? Or is there a difference related to the fact that she is woman? In 1961 Rivers confided to a reporter:

> I don't like to see a woman telling dirty jokes. People say I'm dirty and I always stare at them. My areas are just very "woman's" areas. I have a routine which my husband hates, that for Christmas he gave me a box of Rely tampons. That's not dirty. I think that's very funny. It's such a woman's joke, and it shows what your husband thinks of you....

Besides tampons, Rivers obsesses about other "woman's areas": fat thighs, gynecologists, husband hunting, childbirth, and, of course, jewelry. The aggression in her comedy, mainly directed either toward herself or other women, is based on negative female stereotypes—exaggerated for humor. Her act is peppered with the verbal motifs: "tramp" and "bitch." A "tramp" is gorgeous, sexually promiscuous, and stupid—except when it comes to attracting men.

> I think God divides. If He makes you gorgeous, he makes you stupid. And if He makes you rich, he makes you a bow wow. And most of us are in the middle.

> The most beautiful women in the world are always the dumbest. The most beautiful woman now in the whole world is Bo Derek. Out to lunch as far as I'm concerned! This woman is an idiot! She studied for her pap test! She turned down the role of Helen Keller—she couldn't remember the lines!

Rivers' favorite "tramp" is a comedy character she invented named "Heidi Abramowitz."

> Heidi Abramowitz was such a tramp in high school that when she took off her braces, the football team sent a thank-you note to her dentist.

> A guy once put his hand down the front of her dress, he met two guys coming up.

Real life tramps are famous beauties like Bo Derek, Sophia Loren, nurses (who favor rich old men in oxygen tents) and stewardesses (who reach into overhead luggage racks sans panties: "Sit by the window, you see the earth; sit by the aisle, you see the moon.")

The flip side of a "tramp" is a "bitch"—a tough, clever woman who is out for what she can get. If Heidi Ambrowitz, Bo Derek, and Sophia Loren are tramps, Joan herself is a bitch.

> I love being called a bitch. It means a bright winner. Am I a tramp?
> Don't I wish!

Joan is no dumb blonde, and she is contemptuous toward stupidity. But underneath the contempt is envy—which she is honest enough to admit. Many people harbor a fantasy of being valued simply for their beauty and sex appeal. It would be nice to be successful not because we're smart, tough, or hard workers—but simply because we're desirable females—or males.

Words like "tramp" help us deal with envy toward those who have that much sexual power and experience that much easy pleasure. (As Joan puts it: "Don't I wish!") Her wish is expressed in her spoof photograph of the Blackglama ad. Rivers poses with a mink slipping off one naked shoulder and a cosmeticized, plastic surgerized, retouched, glamorous face and blond coiffure. She is a "wannabe" Marilyn Monroe, the quintessential "tramp."

Inside the album cover is the "bitch"—Rivers' caustic comedy act. Rivers' comedically exaggerated "bitch/tramp" motif, is based on a kernel of of truth about the way people (and especially women) are both over-valued and devalued on the basis of their sex appeal.

> "Bitch" and "tramp" come out of my generation, when there were good girls and bad girls. I think it's funny to call Sophia Loren a tramp. Men are not called tramps—they're studs. In my day, we did what you do now, but we went home afterwards. Some things have changed but there's still a double standard. Women are still bitchy and jealous, in competition for men.

The "bitch/tramp" motif came out of Joan's life as a single woman in the 1950's, living at home with her parents while engaging in secret love affairs and struggling to make it as a stand-up comic. Joan remembers:

> When I started, people thought I was very daring. I was the first to talk about my affair and my mother wanting me to get married. Now values have changed. It's nice to say to a single girl, it's okay not to be

married and live your own life. But I'd love to see my daughter married, and find someone to lean on.

Rivers' first major romance was her passionate liaison with David Fitelson, a history student and a poet, from whom she fled into a "practical," loveless, first marriage with a department store heir. Several years later, Fitelson came back into her life and the affair began again, even more intensely. However, fighting over conflicts of values and goals took their toll and once again the couple separated. When Fitelson swore that he could not live without her, they tried again to make it work—until Rivers discovered that in their three weeks apart, he had gotten one of his old girlfriends pregnant! Furious, Rivers dumped the unnumbered pages of his unfinished doctoral dissertation on the floor and broke off the liaison for good.

Immediately after the break-up, she went on stage in an old raccoon coat he had given her, spoke about the raw pain of the loss, and, feeling the discomfort of the audience, immediately began turning everything into humor.

Do you like this coat?...It was my engagement present...But I knew something was wrong when he told me to wear it in Jersey—during the hunting season.

The idea of turning the raw truth of her own life into comedy came from Rivers' major comedy influence—Lenny Bruce. "Lenny Bruce," she has said, "was a turning point for me as a performer." When Bruce erupted on the comedy scene in the early 1960's, Rivers, who was still outwardly conforming to her parents' values, was initially uninterested in what was rumored to be his pointlessly obscene act. On stage, she never cursed or did sex jokes. But when she went to see his act for herself, it was a revelation. Bruce's onstage persona was a comic anarchist—a molotov cocktail of four-letter words, ethnic epithets, references to all sorts of taboo behavior, and firebomb assault on the hypocrisies of respectable society. To Joan, it was profoundly emancipating. It shone the floodlight of truth on the hypocrisy of her own life, and made her determined to base her act on her own personal truth.

It also gave her a sense of the liberating power of playing with taboo words—using them to shock and then defusing them of their power to wound. In one routine, Bruce did a verbal jazz riff on the words "nigger," "kike," "spic," "mick," "hick," "boogey," "greaseball," and "hunky." He concluded by saying: "The point? That the word's suppression gives it the power, the violence, the viciousness.

If President Kennedy got on television and said, 'Tonight I'd like to introduce the niggers in my Cabinet,' and every time he saw a nigger, he yelled, 'boogeyboogeyboogeyboogeyniggerniggernigger,' till nigger didn't mean anything anymore—you'd never make a 4-year-old nigger cry when he came home from school."

Rivers translated this technique into her own act by using the words "tramp" and "bitch," words that have been used to degrade women, into a funny, repetitive, almost musical motif. Instead of being intimidated by these words, we laugh at them. The difference between Rivers and Bruce is that Bruce articulated the purpose of his routine (to challenge the intimidating power of racist epithets) and Rivers does not. Never does she say that calling a woman a "tramp" or "bitch" is unfair intimidation of women. We are left wondering where she stands. Does she think that this kind of language is demeaning to women? Does she think that women really are either respectable, clever bitches or promiscuous sluts? Or does she just want to play the subject for laughs—and enhance her career as an entertainer?

At the time that Rivers was beginning her stand-up career, there was plenty of resistance to the idea of a woman comic. Self-deprecation eased that resistance—the logic being that if you're doing something women aren't supposed to do, you might be accepted if you show that you don't think much of yourself as a woman. Almost all massively successful stand-up comics were male. Practically the only exceptions were Totie Fields, Phyllis Diller, and Moms Mabley, all of whom presented themselves as very unattractive. Joan looks attractive, but her words reveal her appearance to be phony, a metaphorical drag act for someone who doesn't really fit what a woman is supposed to be. Says Rivers:

> I don't like funny women. I come out of that generation where the woman should be beautiful and sexy and a wonderful flower attached to a man, even though my whole life has been the antithesis of this. To this day, you don't expect a woman to be funny.

A stand-up comic needs to be in control. Rivers has likened her profession to that of a lion tamer, a dominant image, certainly not weak or submissive, traditionally "feminine" virtues. (Interestingly, Mae West, another very funny lady, played the role of a lion tamer in her popular 1933 film *I'm No Angel*.)

Rivers' abrasive comedy style is certainly not ladylike, although her subject areas are female. The dynamic between her insider comedy style—aggressive male—and her outsider subject matter—

victimized female—creates the outsider/insider tension that is at the core of her act. It also reflects her other insider/outsider themes— the private school student whose family couldn't pay the bills, the celebrity who isn't really accepted by the establishment (she's only a semi-legend); and the glamorous performer who is a sexual loser.

Economically and professionally, Joan presents herself as an insider. As a wealthy woman, she is part of the economic establishment. But as a Jew, she is an outsider—never totally part of the mainstream Gentile culture and vulnerable to anti-semitism.

Even as a Jew, she is an outsider/insider. She is a non-observant Jew who established a career in the secular world based on writing and performing sexually frank material, often on the Sabbath. She is therefore outside the expected code of conduct for a traditional Jewish woman,who is supposed to observe the Sabbath, obey religious laws, be subordinate to her husband, and behave with tzinuit, feminine modesty . Most important, as Sarah Blacher Cohen notes in Jewish Wry, she is supposed to enforce *kashrut*, ritual food cleanliness— to keep her home *kosher*—proper and clean.

As a comic, Rivers is in the mainstream of show business careers for Jews, She is also usurping male privilege and violating *tzinuit*, feminine modesty, calling attention to herself by standing center stage and being funny. She verbally violates the concept of *kashrut*, which involves avoiding taboo foods and not mixing meat with dairy and Passover foods with others. Rivers' vulgar jokes do not avoid *unkosher* subjects like sex. By looking like a fashionable matron, she mixes the proper and the profane and makes the respectable Jewish woman, *tref (unkosher)*. Many Jewish jokes play on the secret wish to eat *tref* food (especially pork) without guilt, for example:

> A Jewish man finally saved enough money to travel to Paris. Indulging his curiosity, he ordered a suckling pig. Just as the dish arrived, he saw his rabbi walk in the door. "Oy!" he cried. "You won't believe how they can *potschkeh* (mess) up an apple!"

Like *tref* food, Rivers' tref material is even more delicious presented in the context of her respectable front.

A key quality of Jewish humor is its sense of irony—of the inherent contradiction between life as it should be *(kosher)* and life as it is *(tref)*. As Blacher Cohen notes, central to Jewish experience is the contradiction between being told you are God's chosen people and enduring persecution on earth. Contradiction was built into the very language—Hebrew, a sacred tongue meant for prayers, and Yiddish, the "mother tongue" of European Jews, meant for everyday speech. The Jewish pride in superior intellect is often contradicted by a sense of inferiority toward Gentile insiders, who are held to be more physically attractive, athletic, powerful and confident. Rivers' attack on Bo Derek—the pretty, dimwit, movie star—comes right out of this contradiction.

Rivers' sense of herself as and insider/outsider in many ways reflects Jewish cultural identity as the chosen people/victimized minority group. Unlike Jewish comics who presented more ethnically neutral personae, (for example, Gilda Radner), Rivers presents herself as a modern version of traditional Jewish types. Her celebrity gossip is a Hollywood version of a scandal mongering *yente*. The *yente*, a stock Jewish character dating back to the European *shtetl* (Jewish ghetto), is a coarse, insulting busybody. The *shtetl yente* referred to "Yankele the Hunchback" and "One-Eyed Sadie." Rivers taunts a fat Elizabeth Tailor by saying, "she put on a yellow dress, and thirty kids tried to board her."

The *yente* was often the *schadchen* (matchmaker), making matches with cold-eyed calculation. An ugly man might be introduced to a blind woman with the aside ("The way he looks, and the way she sees—it's a perfect match!") Rivers, true to type, calculates the carats in engagement rings.

The popularity of Jewish comic types and styles testifies to the pervasive Jewish presence in the comedy industry. Jews, who make up barely 2% of the population, have been successful in the comedy field out of all proportion to their numbers. One estimate is that almost 60% of the American humor industry is Jewish. (Even the very WASPy Bob Hope depends on a platoon of writers, many of whom are Jewish.)

American Jewish writers, directors, and performers have evolved a style of comedy that mixes secular and Jewish elements. Like many others, Joan Rivers' on stage persona is an Americanized chicken soup made of traditional Jewish ingredients—canned for mass consumption. Maximizing its market, it is served without Sabbath rituals in the secular environment of nightclubs and television talk shows.

What are these Jewish ingredients? For one thing, her style of delivery incorporates a high degree of emotional spontaneity, expressiveness, and drama. Her mannerisms and diction are Brooklyn-Jewish overlaid with Bel Aire housewife. She shrieks, whispers; glares, denounces, and mock-sobs her response to her audiences and the events of her life.

By comparison, Phyllis Diller and her WASP mentor Bob Hope seem more external, technical, and controlled. When Rivers substituted for Johnny Carson on *The Tonight Show*, her frenetic energy and outrageous questions and comments provided the perfect foil for his WASP blandness and propriety. The WASP code of social courtesy forbids intrusive questions, but Joan queries audience members about their personal lives like the stereotype of the intrusive Jewish mother.

In fact, Joan's onstage character is the JAP—Jewish American Princess—spoiled, materialistic, and pampered. ("I had a Jewish childbirth—they knock you out and wake you up when the hairdresser comes.") She may not fit into WASP ideals of beauty ("I have Jewish thighs"); but she knows how to make the most of her assets:

> Let me see your ring....How'd ja do?...Not bad....You're not Jewish....You are!? You're a Jew and you took that shitty ring? A piece of shit in four prongs. Is your mother alive? Then there's no excuse!

The JAP housewife does not cook, do housework, or serve her husband. What she does well is shop. Measuring the air, Joan tells us that her own hands are the perfect size to hold a credit card!

The stereotypical JAP does not enjoy sex, and Rivers is cynical about catering to the male sexual ego—although it may be necessary to do so to secure material goodies. (Scratching her behind, she looks up at an imaginary male partner, reassures him that he's the best lover she's ever had—and yawns. Then, too bored to concentrate, she examines something on her shoe.)

The JAP is a manicured rebel against the cultural ideal of the self-sacrificing, subordinate female. Smart, rich, and bitchy, she stands (in designer pumps) as Rivers' version of women's liberation.

> I see my image as split. I'm everybody's housewife friend, disgruntled and bitching. It comes out of my feelings about women's liberation. I think of myself as a spy-infiltrator, saying to ladies who have thought about it: "Why should you do housework?" And I don't look like Gloria Steinem. I look like them—which makes it easier to say.

Rivers refusal to play the "nice girl"—even while looking respectable—breaks the taboo against women expressing anger, speaking frankly about sex, or demanding economic power.

> I'm absolutely a feminist. When I started doing stand-up, I played these strip joints, these dives all over the country. At Barnard, I had taken a class with Margaret Mead....I called her and told her I was going to play these crummy clubs and said, "Maybe we can find some-

thing out for women from this." So she said, "Let's do a little survey." She made up a list of questions that I passed out during each of my performances. Then I'd send Mead back the questionnaires with glass marks on them. The questions were "Who do you think should control the income in your family? Who brings in the income? Who stays with the children? Who makes the big decisions? Do you think women should work? Do you think women should have equal say in money investments in the family? " Very basic things. This was the early Sixties. Anyway, when Mead tabulated all the answers, she said, "There's something happening out there, because ladies in Kansas City are saying, "Even though I do work, I don't think I should tell him how to invest the money—or wait a minute, maybe I should tell him."

But like many women in her audience, Rivers stance on women's liberation is ambivalent. She concludes a nightclub act by lugging a tree across the stage, while the men in her orchestra make no offer to help. Panting from the effort, Joan whines about her bad back and curses her own folly in fighting for women's liberation. Only semi-facetiously, Rivers expresses the ambivalence, that she, like many other independent, successful women, feel about giving up female privileges and identity ("a wonderful flower attached to a man) for independent achievement ("my whole life has been the antithesis of this"). Says Rivers:

> Comedy is masculine. To stand up and take control of an audience ver-bally is very difficult. Women are oppressed in childhood and not allowed to do this. Also, women want to be attractive, and comics are not supposed to be that way.

Despite her success in a "masculine" profession, the onstage Rivers advocates the traditional female route to achievement—marrying a rich man. But Rivers herself sees no contradiction:

> Money is important, and one way to get it is through men. Why can't women be liberated and have the fur coats and rings? Get them your-self or get a man to give them to you. Why cook and clean? I'm a woman who's done exactly what she wanted with her life, and an unattractive girl who's pulled herself together.

Joan Rivers' life and act are a hot sauce of spicy contradictions. She's feminist and anti-feminist, insider and outsider, vulgarian and moralist. To Joan, the fact that some people find her comedy offen-sive comes with the territory of being a stand up comic. Says Rivers:

> Shocking people is my job. Good comedy is never "nice"—it deflates hypocrisy. If everybody loves you—never mind your act—get on the shelf and put the oxygen away. It's over.

It seems safe to say that nobody will be putting Joan Rivers away—not for a long time to come. This vulgar, vulnerable virago of comedy and sassy, savvy, survivor of life intends to stick around. As long as there are comedy clubs, theatres, bookstores, and television sets, Joan Rivers, one fat-thighed, fiercely funny lady will be still talking.

Sources

Rivers, Joan, personal interview, conducted at her home in Bel Aire, CA, 1979.

Rivers, Joan, interview, 92nd Street YMHA, New York, New York, 1991.

Rivers, Joan with Richard Meryman, *Enter Talking,* (New York: Delacorte Press, 1986), pp.217, 15, 7, 51, 344, 272-273, 25, 311, 307.

Rivers, Joan, with Richard Meryman, *Still Talking,* (New York: Turtle Baby Books, Random House, 1991) p. 266, 32.

Rivers, Joan, as quoted in "20 Questions: Joan Rivers" *Playboy,* 1961, p.149, 66.

Rivers, Joan, *What Becomes a Semi Legend Most?* Phonodisk, produced by Edgar Rosenberg and Bill Sameth—in association with Diana Thomas, Geffen Records, 1983.)

Rivers, Joan comedy act, Westbury Music Fair, Westbury, Long Island,1980.

"Rushing Rivers," *Vanity Fair,* October, 1990, pp.278, 280, 216.

Stone, Laurie, "Laughing in the Dark," *Village Voice,* September 20, 1988, p.98.

Dumb Doras and
Gawky Gertrudes

No artist exists in isolation. These famous comediennes are part of a continuum—of comedy, of female performers, and of the changing role of women in society. The performing personae created by Lucille Ball, Phyllis Diller, Carol Burnett, and Joan Rivers were influenced by what came before them and by the role of women in their own era. And in turn, they influenced the comediennes who came after them.

The character of Lucy Ricardo was not only a zany version of a 1950s housewife and the product of the talents of Lucille Ball and her staff, it was also a combination of two basic female comedy types—Dumb Dora and Gawky Gertrude. Both types came out of vaudeville and transferred to film, radio, and eventually, television.

An earlier incarnation of the Dumb Dora type was Gracie Allen. Allen and her husband George Burns started out as a "man-woman" act in vaudeville. In most of these acts, the man did the jokes, and the woman fed him set-up lines and entertained by singing, dancing, or just looking pretty. Burns and Allen began the same way. But when Gracie started getting more laughs on her straight lines than George was getting on his jokes, they switched roles.

Apparently, Burns took a lot of teasing from the other male comics for allowing Allen to get the laughs. What may have softened the insult to his masculine pride was the fact that she "played dumb"—unaware that anything she was saying was funny. By 1931, the couple was appearing at the renowned New York Palace Theatre with

109

Eddie Cantor, who invited Allen to appear on his radio show. By the mid-30s, Burns and Allen had their own radio show, *The Adventures of Gracie,* which remained on the air for more than fifteen years. They made several films, and in 1950, premiered their own television series, *The George Burns and Gracie Allen Show,* a domestic comedy still seen in syndication.

A great deal of Gracie Allen's humor (written by male writers), consisted of naive literalism and linguistic confusion:

Gracie: George, my father fell down the stairs with three quarts of liquor.

George: Did he spill it?

Gracie: No, silly. He kept his mouth closed.

Gracie: Guess what, George, my sister had a brand new baby.

George: Boy or girl?

Gracie: I don't know. I can't wait to find out if I'm an aunt or an uncle.

George: They say I'm through as a singer. I'm extinct.

Gracie: You do not.

George: Did the maid drop you on your head when you were a baby?

Gracie: Don't be silly George. We couldn't afford a maid. My mother had to do it.

Gracie: I don't want a husband with money and good looks and personality. I'd rather have George. And I'm not the only one who feels that way. Plenty of women have told me how relieved they are that he's with me.

Easy Aces, a 1930s-1940s radio show, utilized a similar format, with Jane Ace playing the dopey wife to her real-life husband Goodman Ace in this long-running comedy series. Like Gracie Allen, Jane Ace found that her public liked to think of her as a dimwit who mangled the English language. Some of her most engaging mind-twisters are:

That has all the ear-muffs of a dirty dig.

They've been doing that since time immoral.

A thumb-nose description.

You could have knocked me down with a fender.

The Ten Amendments.

And, with an out-of-the-mouths-of-babes wisdom.

Familiarity breeds attempt.

The verbally confused woman is not original with vaudeville or radio. In Richard Sheridan's 1775 play *The Rivals*, the character of Mrs. Malaprop (from the French *mal a propos*—inappropriate) delighted audiences with her mixed up phrases and pronunciations. The character was so popular that her name became part of the language and a "malapropism" denotes any unintentional, amusing verbal confusion.

Mrs. Malaprop established a theatrical type played to the hilt by Gracie Allen and Jane Ace. So adept were Jane and her writers at providing the public with malapropisms that one critic dubbed them "Janeaceisms" and another called her funnier than the original.

Another comedienne malapropster was Carol Channing, a "dumb blonde" given to statements like "Possession is twelve-tenths of the law." Channing was described as "too pretty to be funny, but who can't, apparently, help it." Channing's most famous role was Lorelei Lee, the airhead gold digger who lands a rich husband in *Gentlemen Prefer Blondes*. Her role was taken over in the film version by Marilyn Monroe, the most famous of a long line of pretty, funny-by-accident "dumb blondes" that includes Marie Wilson and and Judy Holliday. (Holliday, who was called the country's "favorite female nitwit" actually had a near-genius I.Q.)

I Love Lucy varied the formula of the dopey, malapropster wife in a few significant ways, which may have accounted for its massive success. First, it included plenty of broad, physical humor—slapstick, mugging, and an extensive use of props. Most slapstick comediennes were homely and unattractive. (A rare exception was Mabel Normand, a silent screen star, who was ready to take a custard pie in her beautiful face—and throw one back). Lucy started out in films as a glamorous extra. But unlike the other showgirls or most Dumb Doras, she was willing to play Gawky Gertrude—fall in mud puddles, get a face full of flour, and be physically funny.

Second, although Lucy is naive and childlike; unlike Gracie and Jane, she is aggressive, manipulative, and determined to bypass the restrictions of her housewife role and lead a more exciting life— preferably in show business. Ball received "tons of letters from people saying they'd love to be able to manipulate their lives the way Lucy does." Underneath her Dumb Dora innocence, Lucy touched a nerve of frustration and restlessness among 1950s housewives. Her aggression made her a more dynamic, exciting heroine.

Lastly, instead of Ricky Ricardo being a standard American husband and straightman (like Richard Denning, Ball's radio spouse on *My Favorite Husband*, the forerunner of *I Love Lucy*), he is a colorful character in his own right. He has a show business career, a passionate "Latin" temperament, and, when under stress, a tendency to lapse into Spanish or give vent to funny English malapropisms. He has some dignity as a husband and head-of-household, but as a foreigner and Latino, he is not given all the authority or stuffiness of an American male. Ricky is part straightman husband and part ethnic comic.

Ethnic comics were a staple of vaudeville since the nineteenth century, when waves of European immigrants flooded American shores. Then and now, American audiences love to laugh at malapropisms of foreigners. In the 1930s and 40s Gertrude Berg played the warmhearted Jewish matriarch Molly Goldberg on the radio show *The Goldbergs* (for which Berg wrote the scripts). The show derived a great deal of humor from the Yiddish flavorings of her dialogue and malapropisms—known as "Mollypropisms"—like "Enter whoever. If it's nobody, I'll call back." (In 1949-51, *The Goldbergs* were on CBS television; but Philip Loeb, who played Molly's husband Jake, was blacklisted during the McCarthy era, and the show was taken off the air.)

Even *I Love Lucy* had an ethnic flavor in the person of Ricky Ricardo. Despite CBS executives' initial reluctance to show Lucy's marriage to a Cuban, they discovered that Arnaz's presence enhanced the popularity of the show by adding color, energy, romance, and a chance for Lucy and her mainly female audience to laugh at a husband with an accent and imperfect English. Ricky tolerated the needling because he knew that he was allowed to play the adult member of the couple, the father figure to Lucy's child/wife.

The popularity of the Dumb Dora type has extended even beyond women portraying childlike adults. Comediennes have, in far greater numbers than men, portrayed comic characters who were children. Peter Pan, a magical little boy in the play by Philip Barrie, is traditionally played by adult women.

In the United States, one of the first female entertainers to achieve national stature as a comedienne was the ever-youthful Lotta Crabtree. At the peak of her career in the 1890s, she was the highest paid actress of her day. She sang (often parodies), danced, did plenty of physical comedy—and even yodeled. Throughout her career and well into her forties, she played many child parts—boys as well as girls. Even when she pulled up her skirts to show her knees or rolled off a couch with her petticoats flying, she did so with an air of innocence that made it seem wholesome.

One of the most famous child characters was "Baby Snooks," created by Fanny Brice. Brice, a brilliant musical comic, made her initial success with coon songs, Yiddish dialect material, slapstick take-offs of famous beauties and historical figures, and the torch song "My Man" based on her obsessive relationship with her ne'er do well husband, con man Nicky Arnstein.

However, her greatest success came in the second stage of her career, when she presented "Baby Snooks" on the radio in 1930s and 1940s. The show was enormously successful, and very quickly "Baby Snooks" became the only part Brice played. In fact, she successfully portrayed "Baby Snooks" on the radio until her death at fifty-nine, in 1961.

Audience resistance to adult female funniness or sexuality was neatly bypassed by presenting material in the guise of a child. Brice commented:

> We'd be ready to rehearse and they'd say: "You can't do this, you can't do that. This will offend and that will not sound nice." And I knew this couldn't happen with a baby. Because what can you write about a child that has to be censored?

One of "Baby Snooks" trademarks was a long, loud "Wa-a-ah!" and "Why-y-y Daddy?"; and Brice always played the character in a baby voice. In much the same way Ball played Lucy as a child/wife, complete with a mannerisms like a "Gabloots Voice" and wailing "Rickyyyy!" But while Lucy at least looked like an adult woman, even dressing in snug outfits that showed her excellent figure, Brice became more and more absorbed by Snooks, sometimes even conducting interviews in a baby voice.

The tradition of women playing child characters has continued into modern times. Lily Tomlin began playing "Edith Ann," a snotty, but lovable five-year-old on the late 1960s television variety show *Laugh In*. Tomlin subsequently sued the program for rights to the character, and later released recordings featuring Edith Ann.

Gilda Radner originated "Judy Miller," a hyperactive six-year-old in the late 1970's on *Saturday Night Live*. After a scene in which she and Larraine Newman played two little girls in party dresses, the actresses remarked, "When will they let us grow up?" In the 1980s Whoopi Goldberg starred in a one-woman Broadway show, portraying a variety of funny, poignant characters. She made her strongest, anti-racist and pro-choice statements in the character of a little girl and a thirteen year old.

It is true that some male comedians play child characters—for example, Red Skelton's "Junior." However, it is nowhere near as common among male comedians as it is among female performers. (None of the male comedians on *Laugh-In* or *Saturday Night Live* played children.) And rarely have male comics continued to play child characters into late middle-age as did Crabtree and Brice. Even when comediennes play characters who are not literally children (i. e. Lucy Ricardo), childlike elements are often prominent. The best-known contemporary comedienne who has based a career on an adorable childlike persona is Goldie Hawn. In 1967, Hawn was a struggling dancer who was supporting herself by by performing in go-go joints, when she was cast for a new TV show called *Good Morning, World*. She was spotted by producer George Schlatter, who thought she would be right for his new show—*Rowan and Martin's Laugh In*. He gave her three shows to prove herself. During one rehearsal, she blew her simple line three times straight. Mortified, she broke into a giggle.

> When I read the cue cards, I was so nervous, I got mixed up and started to laugh, "Oh please, could you start over again, please?" There was George in his booth, watching me and saying, "Not on your life! Keep going Goldie." And so my character grew out of that—an extension of my real reaction to my own frailties.

To keep Goldie's mix-ups and resultant giggles spontaneous, the crew devised tricks to throw her off-balance. But like the Dumb Dora comediennes before her, Hawn found playing an adorable nitwit increasingly burdensome.

> *Laugh-In* was a great training ground. We were an ensemble, and I'm comfortable in ensembles—it's what I grew up on. But as the years went on it got harder. I had to be consistently one character. There was no room for anything else.

The character that Hawn created on *Laugh-In* included elements of the go-go dancer she had been—played with a dotty innocence reminiscent of Gracie Allen. Hawn appeared in a bikini—which showed off her dancer-slim figure—and wore her hair in a short, pixyish style. Her body was covered with amusing slogans and pictures in the body painting style that was was popular with the "flower children" of the late 1960s. Like Crabtree's rolling off an 1890s couch in childish glee and "accidentally" pulling up her petticoats, Hawn's bikini-plus-body painting enticed her audience with hints of nudity, offered in a spirit of childlike fun. She was not simply a blonde in a bikini but a canvas for silly graffiti—a kind of walking toy.

Like a child undone by stage fright, Hawn was reduced to giggles by the need to perform. Her helpless laughter betrayed the same childish confusion that had led dizzy Gracie Allen and Jane Ace to lapse into amusing malapropisms. Her humor was not created by conscious wit, as in the case of say, Joan Rivers or Phyllis Diller, but by her charming incompetence.

Hawn's success on *Laugh-In* was also the product of fortuitous timing. In the 1950s, television comediennes usually played housewives. Lucille Ball, Gracie Allen, Harriet Nelson, and Joan Davis, along with a host of others, played comedic versions of adult wives and mothers. Even a sketch comedienne like Imogene Coca usually appeared on *Your Show of Shows* as Sid Caesar's wife.

But by the late 1960s, the nuclear family, along with other traditional values was in upheaval. The stable, patriarchal structures of both family and society as a whole were being questioned. The counter-culture was permeating the mainstream with ideals of freedom, spontaneity, sensuality, anti-rational ecstasy (often induced by drugs), and rebellion against authority and the ideal of disciplined, hard work. The feminist movement had yet to be solidified, and women as a group were not yet organized and demanding to be taken seriously as independent adults. In fact, the whole notion of serious adulthood was under question. The adults (who had presumably brought the country the Vietnam war, racial discrimination, and sexual repression) were viewed as morally corrupt and not much fun. In place of respect for their supposedly wiser elders, the under thirty-year-olds of the baby boom elevated their own "youth culture." *Laugh-In* domesticated the excesses of the youth culture for the consumption of the home audience. The title of the show was a play on "Be-In," the large-scale, free-spirited, hippie-type gatherings (complete with body-painting) that were popular at the time. In keeping with the contemporary mood, *Laugh-In* moved along at a frenetic pace, slapping together irreverent skits, jokes, and sight gags, often edited with the blitzkrieg cutting of a television commercial. The cast members danced free-style to rock music. (Hawn, the former go-go dancer, was particularly good at this.) The overall mood was one of good-humored disorder, a kind of free-form craziness. If the jungles of Vietnam had left Americans holding a tiger by the tail,

Laugh-In was a kind of cheery zoo with Goldie Hawn as its kittenish mascot.

The youth culture viewed domesticity—and domestic comedy—with suspicion. *Laugh-In* may have needed a funny sweetheart, but she was not to be a housewife. Enter Goldie Hawn, the girlfriend/flower child. Her voice is high and squeaky. Her body is adolescent. Her eyes roll like big, blue marbles and pop open like Jacks-in-the box. When she feels embarrassed, she nibbles her lower lip with bunny teeth and shrugs adorably. To show friendliness, she flutters her hand in the manner of a child taught to wave "bye-bye." When she's bewildered, she breaks into shrieking giggles. Other *Laugh-In* cast member may say funny things or play a variety of funny sketch characters. Giggling Goldie, with her eponymously colored hair falling over her saucer-sized eyes, simply is funny.

Laugh-In made Goldie Hawn an instantly recognizable type—the dumb blonde as flower child. She misread lines, mispronounced words, even hit herself over the head with an over-sized foam mallet, grinning "sock it to me." Goldie was sexy, innocent, and fun—a confection of cuddly confusion. No wonder audiences took her to heart and she was able to move quickly from being a member of the *Laugh-In* ensemble to starring in her own television special *(Pure Goldie)* and into feature films.

Hawn's first major screen role was as Walter Matthau's sweetly suicidal mistress in the 1969 comedy Cactus Flower. Hawn's role was not the lead, and Lucille Ball was offered the starring part—that of the spinster who eventually blooms into love like a "cactus flower." Ball shrewdly refused the role. Having seen Hawn on *Laugh-In* and calculated the effect of the blonde comedienne's personality on an audience, the older comedienne surmised that "Goldie would walk away with the picture."

As it turned out, Ball was quite right. Hawn's first major screen role resulted in an Academy Award for best supporting actress. Hawn's reaction to the award was ambivalent:

> I felt empty. I wanted to win for working hard. I like to sweat. That performance was just a drop in the bucket.

In her subsequent films, Hawn was rarely challenged to create anything of depth. For the next few years, she starred in a series of financially successful light comedies, playing a sweet, sexy, abused innocent who goes through a series of farcical misadventures, but with the help of the right man, lands on her feet.

The film that established her as an executive producer as well as a major star was the 1980 comedy *Private Benjamin,* which grossed $100 million world wide and spun off a successful television series. Hawn, who first won public notice as a 1960s dumb blonde/flower child, created a vehicle that responded to the feminism of the late 1970s and early 1980s. *Private Benjamin* showed the seamy, painful side of Dumb Dora femininity and the need for female independence. Private Benjamin. w as a farce with a feminist message.

The film stars Hawn as Judy Benjamin, adorable, empty-headed, and trained for a life of homemaking and shopping. She survives a brief marriage to a family-approved husband (who uses her as a sexual convenience); a sadistic C.O. in the army (which she impulsively joined in the mistaken belief that basic training resembled Club Med); and an unfaithful, patronizing fiancé (whom she punches out at the altar) to emerge alone and triumphant—the independent new woman.

The Judy Benjamin character is a variant of the dizzy blond Hawn played on *Laugh-In* with the addition of personal history and sexual politics. Hawn retains her trademark giggle, sweet sexiness, and confusion. But, while exaggerated, Judy Benjamin has human dimension and feelings. The sketch character Hawn presented on *Laugh-In* was a figure of innocently sexy, goofy fun—a kind of blonde Disney chipmunk. This character may have been suitable for the brief sketches of a variety show, but to serve as the protagonist of a full-length narrative, she needed more complexity.

In *Private Benjamin,* Hawn's charm is turned against her by exploitive males. She adopts a sexually compliant Dumb Dora persona and sells herself into marriage. She denies her own abilities and worth in order to gain approval from a patriarchal world. (When the truth of her situation hits her, she confronts both her father and daddylike fiancé: "Don't call me stupid!")

The humiliations of *Laugh-In* were painless and farcical (being doused by water or hit over the head with styrofoam mallets). Besides, everyone in the cast was equally at the mercy of a slapstick universe. But as Judy Benjamin, Hawn is personally and uniquely subject to abuse of her feelings and sexuality. In short, Hawn's highly externalized, farcical sketch character is given vulnerability, a feminist context, and the potential for growth.

The cruelty of some of the humor in *Private Benjamin,* particularly in connection with Hawn's sexual abuse, was startling to those who had associated Hawn with frothy comedy. But Hawn herself was aware of the seamy side of show business—from the customers who had exhibited themselves and masturbated while she performed as a go-go dancer to producers who tried to trick her onto a casting couch. She had also been through two difficult marriages—her first ending in a divorce in which she had to make a financial settlement of $75,000, and her second, which was shaky during the production of *Private Benjamin,* and ended in divorce shortly after the release of the motion picture. (Her third long-term relationship, to live-in boyfriend actor Kurt Russell, is apparently far happier and on more solid ground.)

In fact, it was Hawn who fought for the painful realism of some of the sex scenes—particularly the scene early in the movie where her second husband pressures her into having sex with him in the back seat of a car during their wedding reception. Hawn comments:

> I wanted the scene in there because I wanted to demonstrate something about Judy's character—that basically she was someone who didn't have much self-esteem. She wasn't able to say, "NO! I don't want to do this. I'm in my wedding gown. It's our wedding night. I'm embarrassed" What she valued most was having a man take care of her. She was prepared to be a doormat.

> There was no tenderness involved, so the scene showed his character and hers. She pleaded briefly, realized "Okay, I have to do this," and then she went down out of the frame. The script was written for me. I have a clear vision of what I wanted.

Director Howard Zieff noted that Hawn wished to take the graphic harshness of the scene even further.

> Goldie wanted to linger on that scene for a long time. And she wanted to let the audience see the back of her head in her husband's lap. I objected to that, and I guess I was afraid of the scene anyway, in that I didn't want the audience to squirm during it.

It seems clear that Hawn wanted to make a personal, feminist point, despite her director's uneasiness about how the audience would take such a scene in a film that was billed as a comedy. The graphic sexuality and painful humiliation of the heroine take the film beyond the fluffy farce that had been the formula of the "Goldie Hawn films." And in fact, when *Private Benjamin* was made into a television situation comedy, the producers of the tv series extracted only the farcical mid-section of the film (where spoiled Judy tries to adjust to army life), left out the tougher, more feminist parts, and lightened up the Judy Benjamin character.

The misfit-in-the-army was a well-established formula well before *Private Benjamin*. Earlier examples of the same genre are *Never Wave at a WAC*, a1952 Rosalind Russell vehicle about a Washington hostess who winds up in the army; *Operation Mad Ball*, *M*A*S*H*, and *Charlie Chaplin's Shoulder Arms*. But where these other films had played the subject for laughs, Hawn infuses the formulaic army comedy with sexual vulnerability.

Hawn's later films are often variations of the *Private Benjamin* format—abused, adorable, innocently sexy Hawn fights her way to respect in the macho worlds of a World War II defense plant *(Swing Shift)*, Washington politics *(Protocol)*; or high school football *(Wildcats)*. In her more recent films Hawn, now in her late forties, has allowed herself to hint at the some of the toughness that provided the infrastructure for her girlish charm. It remains to be seen if audiences will accept a tarnished Goldie.

Allowing her reel-life to reflect her real-life survival skills is a risky move for Hawn, who has built a career on her childlike charm. At 5'6", Goldie Hawn, is about average female height. But to emphasize her girlish daintiness, Hawn often cast herself against much larger co-stars. In *Swing Shift*, her best girlfriend is played by the statuesque Christine Lahti. In *Wildcats*, she plays the coach of a ghetto football team, whose muscular heft sets off her babydoll delicacy. In *Private Benjamin* she joins a squadron of tall, male paratroopers who line up for inspection. The camera, which has been panning along a line of male paratroopers, must suddenly drop down to bring "tiny" Goldie into the frame.

Hawn also used editing to comment on her good-girl character and create humor. Hawn, who was herself half-Jewish, used film montage to play Judy Benjamin's respectable Jewish background for laughs. Says Hawn:

> Here's an example of how you can destroy or create a moment through timing. When I kissed Armand Assante under the street lamp in *Private Benjamin*, he was telling me about himself, and I was hesitant about being with him. When he finally said, "And I'm Jewish," they cut to my scream, to my orgasm. Now that is a funny cut. However, when it was first cut, it was not funny, because there was too much space between "I'm Jewish" and the orgasm. Those few millimeters of a second were the difference between whether it was funny or not. Because you've got "I'm Jewish" Beat. Beat. Beat. Arghh!"— see, it has to come right on top of the line.

Comic timing is also crucial in the progression within scenes. Hawn, who was trained as a dancer, is very conscious of the importance of timing in building a comic effect within a scene. Says Hawn:

> Comedy is like music. I remember working with an actor who couldn't get the scene, couldn't get the timing. So I beat it out with my hands. It was like percussion, so he could understand the arch of the scene and the power it had to have. It's as if I hear the beats in my head.

Hawn's description of comic timing resembles that of Phyllis Diller, who also compared comedy to music and noted that many comics were musicians. Diller was trained as a concert pianist, while Hawn studied dance. In both disciplines, the performer counts beats and plays an instrument or moves within a specific time frame. Probably as a consequence of their training, both Diller and Hawn discuss their comic technique in terms of rhythm and timing.

Unlike Diller, Hawn also developed her comic timing as part of an ensemble, reacting to her fellow actors, as did Carol Burnett and Lucille Ball. Hawn's character is also much closer to that of Ball. Unlike Carol Burnett and Phyllis Diller, Hawn usually plays an attractive woman, and her background as a dancer parallels Ball's background as a showgirl. However, Hawn's on-screen sexuality is more overt than that of Lucy. Some of the difference may be accounted for by the fact that Hawn and Ball are very different physical types. Hawn is shorter and provocatively cute, with a high-pitched voice and a girlish giggle. Ball was statuesque and voluptuous, with a deep voice and a manner that was sufficiently aggressive to have her cast as a "tough girl" in B movies. Hawn's film roles often called for her to assume suggestive poses and wear scanty costumes, or, as occurs in the bathtub scene in *Wildcats*, nothing at all.

What allows Hawn to retain her innocence is the cuddly nature of her appeal. It's hard to imagine Lucy Ricardo being overtly provocative. Ball's height and deep voice would make her sexiness too formidable. But Hawn's kittenish appeal is more playful and less threatening.

The fact that Hawn's characters are more overtly sexual than Lucy Ricardo also reflects changing social mores. No matter what Ball did in her private life, both her image and that of Lucy Ricardo conformed to 1950s standards of female virtue. But Hawn became famous in the sexually frank 1960s. Both her personal arrangements (for the last several years she has been co-habiting with actor Kurt Russell, with whom she has a child) and the characters she plays reflect a contemporary permissiveness. In fact, within a contemporary context, Hawn's life and screen roles are relatively respectable—it's simply that "good girls" now do more freely and frankly what only "bad girls" used to do.

To clarify public acceptance of women's roles vis-à-vis sexuality, motherhood, and power, let's take a look at situation comedy heroines from different eras. In the 1950s, the word "pregnant" was considered too risque for *I Love Lucy*, even though the on-air birth of baby Ricky (to the respectably married Ricardos) attracted a 71.7 percent of American television homes. In the 1970s, *The Mary Tyler Moore Show* portrayed a single,working woman with boyfriends and a descreetly handled sex life. In 1992, on *Murphy Brown,* a single female boss had a baby which she planned to raise on her own without any help from the father, whose identity was uncertain. And in a 1994 episode of *Grace Under Fire,* when a married woman wants to get pregnant, we are treated to jokes about eggs, sperm, and fertility clinics. ("Life is unfair. I had lots of sex and I can't get pregnant.")

Some of the difference between Lucy Ricardo and the Hawn characters also relates to their genres—situation comedy vs. theatrical films. Television programs are meant to entertain home audiences so they'll buy sponsors' products. Lucy was expected to act respectably and support family values, not be sexually provocative or model unwholesome habits. Lucy does, however, smoke, probably because *I Love Lucy* was sponsored by the Philip Morris Tobacco Company, and smoking in the 1950s was not viewed as unhealthy. Alcohol was less respectable and liquor companies did not sponsor situation comedies. Predictably, Lucy is so naive about drinking that she becomes intoxicated on a spiked medication without noticing the alcoholic content. Although Goldie Hawn first came to public notice on television, she quickly moved into feature films, where she achieved her greatest success. Unlike situation comedies, theatrical films are not a domestic medium. Unless specifically designed for that purpose, they are not expected to provide family entertainment. In fact, the mass audience for a most blockbuster Hollywood films is late adolescent/early adult (which accounts for the popularity of action films). Films are less subject to censorship. In fact, like a nightclub act, films are expected to provide what cannot be seen on television.

An "X" rating may be a commercial handicap, but so is a "G" rating for everything but children's films. Some titillation in the form of sex (and/or violence) is usually required to recoup the considerable investment of a Hollywood feature.

Since films do not have to please sponsors or be tame enough to enter family living rooms, you might expect them to be more adventurous than television. However, the need to justify the initial investment with bankable stars and audience pleasing plots often sharply limits the casting and subject matter of most commercial films. Network and public television, despite its greater censorship, has a broader audience base, and sometimes tackles more varied subject matter (excepting the graphic depiction of sex and violence) than do feature films. And cable television, though it is constrained to a more limited budget, is even more free to experiment.

Goldie Hawn, who achieved stardom in commercial feature films, portrays characters whose sexual behavior, including mild nudity, is far more overt than that of a situation comedy heroine. However, in keeping with her image as a "nice girl," she is never really graphic or shocking. The financial consideration of recouping an investment on a "Goldie Hawn picture" and perhaps her own personal inclinations or unwillingness to tamper with a successful formula have limited her choice of vehicle and the characters she portrays.

If we imagine the development of female comedy styles as a kind of tree, then one branch might be the dumb blondes and dizzy dames who are pursued and patronized by men. Forking off in an opposite direction is a sister branch: the homely muggers and inept manchasers who are rejected by men. If the Dumb Doras deny their intellect, then the Gawky Gertrudes deny their sexuality—or at least fail to attract male romantic attention. The more interesting Dumb Doras sometimes transcend their stereotype; for example, Goldie Hawn's better films reveal the vulnerable underside of being a bubble-headed sex object. The more interesting Gawky Gertrudes grow past their muggery; for example, Carol Burnett was able to infuse her roles with warmth, vulnerability, and insight. But even though the more gifted performers were able to ring some changes on their "type," it was through use of their established "type" that the performers were able to achieve public acceptance and express their talents.

An early example of the Gawky Gertrude was Marie Dressler, whose antics delighted audiences on stage and in feature films. Her career spanned the late 19th century to the 1930s, and in the early '30s this "aging, ugly, bulky lady" was a bigger draw than Greta Garbo. Once, at the annual ball of the Newspaper Women's Club of New York, she good-naturedly allowed Will Rogers to give the crowd a laugh and avoid offending any real beauties by picking her out as the most beautiful woman in the room.

Despite a comedy style that some critics called coarse or vulgar, she insisted that what she did was "decent, respectable" and done with "refinement." She mixed pratfalls with pathos and had a keen sense of the irony of her success as a homely woman making it in a profession where the first requirement was supposed to be a pretty face, and a "born serious" person who made a living making an audience laugh. She summed up her own paradox in an autobiography, which she titled *The Life Story of an Ugly Duckling.*

Fanny Brice, another "ugly duckling," headlined in the *Ziegfeld Follies*—a showcase for swans—beautiful young showgirls. In a comic comment on her situation, Brice performed a hilarious send-up of a fan dancer and an awkward ballet dancer who stumbled her way through "The Dying Swan." (A popular episode of *I Love Lucy* featured a version of Brice's routine—Lucy's amusingly ungainly "swan ballet.") Like Carol Burnett, Fanny Brice was possessed of a funny face, an attractive figure, an aptitude for slapstick, and a fascination with glamour. Like Burnett, she lampooned famous beauties from history and Hollywood. And again, like Burnett and many other comediennes who mocked their appearance, she had plastic surgery—Burnett's on her chin and jaw, and Brice's on her "Jewish" nose. (Dorothy Parker, who was herself Jewish, caustically remarked: "Fanny Brice cut off her nose to spite her race.")

Like Burnett and Brice, Judy Canova combined broad, physical slapstick with singing. She was actually a classically trained coloratura soprano with a three-octave range; but the singing part of her act featured spoofs of country-western tunes, including yodeling. Juliet Canova (her original name) was descended from a wealthy, cultivated family. At her mother's suggestion, she and her brother Leon (re-named Zeke) and sister Diana (re-named Annie) performed a hillbilly act during the Depression. When Juliet/Judy went off on her own, she continued her hillbilly character.

Canova wore her hair in long pigtails, covered with a straw hat. She dressed in a checkered jacket and carried a battered suitcase. Her comic persona was the inept, man-chasing hillbilly. She was used as a rug, was frozen in a refrigerator, and took dozens of pratfalls—including one down a fire-escape. Her gags played off her own "ugliness":

When I was four years old, my father took me to the zoo.

What happened?

They rejected me.

countrified lustiness:

> When Pomeroy started kissin' me, the ushers had to take down the sign "20 Degrees Cooler Inside." The popcorn started shootin' holes in the candy bars.

and supposed ignorance:

> Do you sing Faust?
>
> Sure. I sing Faust or slow.
>
> Have you ever been to Cannes?
>
> No, but I had an uncle who was in the jug.

Her dim-wittedness was capsulized in the titles of her movies *Scatterbrain, Puddin'head, Sleepytime Gal,* and *Lazybones.* She also let fly with a few of her own insults. When a fellow performer said, "I'm only human," Judy replied, "You're exaggerating." Her bumpkin stage personality was so successful was that she was dubbed the "Duse of the Sticks."

Minnie Pearl (born Sarah Ophelia Colley) also got a lot of mileage out of playing the homely hillbilly. Dressed in a yellow organdy dress, white stockings, scuffed shoes, black purse, and a straw hat with a $1.98 price tag dangling off on edge, she greeted audiences with an enthusiastic" "Howdee! I'm just so proud to be hyere!"

She debuted at the *Grand Old Opry* in 1940, became a a popular fixture of the show, and appeared on the radio and television version of the Opry, as well as on NBC's *Swinging Country* and *Hee-Haw.* Pearl hailed from Grinders Switch, Tennessee, Colley's fantasy version of a small southern town populated by colorful characters:

> Grinders Switch is so small, you don't read the paper to find out who is doin' what—you already know that—but to find out if they got caught.
>
> A man came to Grinders Switch and said to my Uncle Maybob, "You lived here all your life?" And Uncle Maybob says, "Not yet."
>
> My brother was draggin' a chain, and someone says, "Why are you pullin' that long chain?" And my brother says, "You ever try pushin' one of these things?"

(Sophisticated audiences who may think Minnie Pearl's stories of Grinders Switch are corny or out-of-date, need only to look at their modern incarnations. Pearl plucks the same American heartstrings as the tongue-in-cheek nostalgia of some of today's popular shows, for example, Garrison Keeler's radio-village of Lake Wobegon or *Northern Exposure*—network television's gently satiric version of small-town Alaska.)

Like Canova, Colley came from a family that stressed education— her parents' home was the best-stocked library in town. Said Colley, "It was drilled into my head when I made a grammatical error, and then I go into a business where I commercialize on nothing but grammatical errors. It's a kind of paradox."

The Depression and death of her father ended her career at the exclusive finishing school where she was studying acting. The drama teacher told Colley she had no sense of humor and discouraged her comic antics. But Colley had inclined toward comedy ever since at the age of eight, she overheard a friend of her mother describe her as a "plain, little thing." Colley remembers: "I didn't think I was very pretty, and I did it to get attention."

After leaving school, Colley taught piano, drama, and dance. To earn money, she toured with a country musical show and picked up the country stories and expressions that became the basis for Minnie Pearl's rural character. Says Colley:

> "Minnie" and "Pearl" are great country names. I put them together because southern country people as a rule use double names.

Colley usually spoke about Minnie Pearl in the third person, as a kinder, gentler, countrified,version of what she'd like to be.

> I like to talk about her because she is warm and friendly; and she has all the qualities I wish I had—no prejudice, she never gossips, she never bears false witness, she never does any of the things you are not supposed to do. She is pretty near perfect, you know, and I kind of like her. She's nicer than I am and funnier. And she doesn't have the problems or hang-ups I have.

Minnie Pearl's gentle, country humor suited her Opry audience, and grew out of Colley's encounter with rural people. By way of contrast, Phyllis Diller's rapid-fire gags were tailored to the impatient crowds in urban nightclubs and modeled on the big-time show business act of Bob Hope. But aside from their stylistic differences, these comediennes have a lot in common. Both Colley and Diller play highly artificial, costumed characters who bear little resemblance to their own cultivated backgrounds (which include a strong awareness of proper grammar and training in classical piano); both felt themselves unattractive as youngsters and grew up to play awkward "Gawky Gertrude" types; both invented and used a cast of fictional characters in their acts (Diller's Fang, Mother-in-Law, and Sexpot Sister and Pearl's assorted relatives in Grinders Switch); and both are basically heartland American WASPs (Pearl is southern; and Diller is mid-Western). Although they did solo acts, their humor is based on a theatrical character. Diller calls her performance a "proscenium act"; and Minnie Pearl is Colley's variation on a well-known theatrical type (also played by Judy Canova)—the naive mountain-girl.

The hillbilly "type" was often portrayed as man-crazy—a key feature of Ado Annie, the female, comic supporting role in the musical *Oklahoma*. (Ado Annie's signature song is "I'm Just a Girl Who Can't Say No.") Burnett,who played the role to great effect in her college production of Oklahoma, went on to portray a ludicrous man-chaser in *Once Upon A Mattress*, in the comic ballad "I Made a Fool of Myself Over John Foster Dulles," and in sketches on *The Gary Moore Show* and her own variety show.

I Love Lucy also used a variant of the hillbilly manchaser. In one episode, Lucy and Ethel pretend to be their husbands' blind dates, dress up as hillbillies, and chase their husbands around the room. However, when their husbands discover the trick and chase after them, Lucy and Ethel quickly beat a ladylike retreat.

(The notion of a wife being sexually aggressive was untenable on 1950s television. Even Joan Davis, who had made a name for herself by portraying an inept, man-hungry, slapsticker was toned down for her television series *I Married Joan*—a less successful version of *I Love Lucy*. Davis portrayed a housewife who concocted hare-brained schemes and mugged. But as a lady, she never acted as the sexual pursuer.)

If the comedy of Pearl/Diller/Canova/Burnett/Ball/Davis is based on exaggerated southern or middle-American WASP characters, that of Joan Rivers is more realistic, intimate and directly connected to her own urban, ethnic experience. As Rivers has stated, her strongest influence was Lenny Bruce,who stressed developing comedy out of one's own personal pain and truth. The Bruce/Rivers strain has been a major influence on today's stand-up comics, for example, Joy Behar. Like Bruce/Rivers, Behar's comedy is urban, abrasive, and ethnic. Bruce and Rivers are Jewish; Behar (born Josephine Occhiuto) is Italian—although her "Noo Yawk" accent, Brooklyn mannerisms, and surname (taken from her ex-husband, a Sephardic Jew) convince many fans that she is Jewish. Behar jokes:

Last year I got a call. "Happy Chanukah." I said "Ma, I'm *not Jewish.*"

If Colley populated her comedy routines with the rural characters of Minnie Pearl's Grinders Corners, Behar peppers her act with references to her own Italian family and Brooklyn neighborhood, where "the layered look was an apron over a sweater."

One of Joy's favorite relatives is Aunt Rose, who plies her Thanksgiving table with soup, antipasto, lasagna, frito misto, eggplant parmigian and candied yams (the yams she got from *Father Knows Best)* Then one year, she decided to cut out the soup, so now she says, "We don't eat heavy like we used to."

The neighborhood busybody is Sadie Catalano, who reports:

> Only a hail of bullets marred the fesitivites as wedding bells rang for Carmela Rose Cartucci.

Joy's own mother was a seamstress, her father was a trucker for the teamsters. Says Behar, "I'm only one generation away from banging laundry on the rocks in Calabria."

The closeness of Behar to her own ethnic, working-class background is one of the key differences between her and Rivers, who comes from a socially ambitious, Larchmont doctor's family and studs her act with comic gossip about the rich and famous. Both comediennes host talk shows that feature lots of warm, personal chat, and both are free with their opinions and advice. But where Rivers devotes a segment of her WPIX show to celebrity scandal, Behar dedicates much of her WABC call-in radio show to her listeners' disgruntled views of politics and says, "Rivers' schtick is 'get the ring, get the husband.' Mine is 'get your independence' and jokes, "I want a man in my life, but not in my house."

Unlike Rivers, whose career was managed for twenty-two years by husband Edgar Rosenberg, Behar began her career as a divorcée and maintains it sans husband. As she sarcastically confides to her audience: "I'm divorced. Hard to believe, isn't it?"

Behar's cynical view of marriage (she does have a long-term boyfriend) runs counter to the dependent Dumb Dora stance toward men. Like Gawky Gertrude, she concocts comedy out of her failure to achieve a bathing beauty physique.

> I hate to exercise. I joined a health club. I haven't gone, but I joined. I gave them $500—let them go!

Like Gertrude she is strong and aggressive, but unlike her Gawky forebear, she is not an inept man-chaser, but rather a practical materialist whose ideal date is:

A tall, skinny Jewish guy with an astigmatism. The kind who when
you say Leonard, get the check—he jumps!

In fact, Behar's version of Gawky Gertrude is the modern wit and
wisecracker, a strong, smart, aggressive woman who throws her
unladylike attitude "in your face."

Martha Raye, whose comedy career peaked before the 1960s and
whose comedy was more physical than verbal, did not have easy
recourse to a modern feminist stance. Her aggressive, boisterous
comic style and generous mouth, made up to accentuate its size,
brought her fame, fortune, fans and ridicule. Critics called her "stri-
dently funny," "the lady with the mouth," "rubber mouth," "tunnel
mouth," and "mammoth cave." Said Raye:

> I know I've got a big mouth. I guess I've won a lot of fans by stretching
> it to make it look even bigger than it is. That's swell and I'm grateful.
> You're lucky in this business if people like you for any reason, even
> the size of your mouth.

When another reporter asked if she minded the "big mouth deal,"
she replied: "No. I'm a clown. Clowns are singular. To be a clown is a
gift." Raye cited the funny-faced Marie Dressler as her "ideal" But in
a pensive moment, she admitted:

> Ask any girl what she'd rather be than beautiful, and she'll say more
> beautiful. Having your worst feature get the spotlight doesn't help
> much when you look at it that way.

The "big mouth" label may have had to do with an exaggeration
of the effect of Raye's singing style. She started out as a band singer,
and her mode of high-volume, power belting required her to open
her mouth very wide. This vocalism, combined with her raucous,
comic style, and her taste for "blue" humor (which she performed in
nightclubs, on military tours, and for her own off-stage amusement)
led critics to exaggerate aspects of her appearance in the direction of
the unfeminine and bizarre.

(Carol Burnett, though less coarse, has said that she "came out of
the era of the muggers" and was similarly labeled. On one question-
answer session with her studio audience, someone asked if her
mouth was insured. Burnett laughed and answered, "There isn't
enough money!")

Raye scored a success in films with her brand of broad clowning.
Despite her beautiful legs and voluptuous figure, audiences refused
to accept her in glamour roles (although she would sometimes play

the man-chaser). Her innate boisterousness tended to surface—even when she was dressed in the furs and gowns she loved wearing.

> I've got to admit it comes natural to me to be noisy when I'm excited or having a good time...nobody knows better than I do that voices and faces like mine don't go with high hats.

Charlie Chaplin, who starred opposite Raye in Monsieur Verdoux, advised her to capitalize on the contrast and "Be coiffed and grand. Look as well as you can. That way, when you take a pratfall, it's really funny." (Like Raye, Burnett combined elegance and slapstick and said, "The better dressed you are when things happen to you, the funnier it is.")

Raye's 1950s television series was in the top ten of the ratings, and one critic called her "the country's number one comedienne...the unqualified queen of buffoon." But her ratings began to slide and her personal troubles, including the dissolution of her fifth marriage and a charge of home-wrecking by the wife of her new boyfriend, undermined her career and resulted in a suicide attempt. She recovered and went on to appear on television and films, and spent four months of every year on unpaid military tours, entertaining, visiting, and occasionally nursing the wounded. (Bette Midler's film For The Boys, was based on an unauthorized version of Raye's life.)

Perhaps because of her rowdy humor or turbulent private life (including seven husbands), critics were often vicious. Raye sued one magazine to prevent them from publishing a photo of herself next to a chimpanzee—both with their mouths wide open.

The tendency of critics to attack comediennes on the basis of their looks applied even to Imogene Coca, In 1939, Collier's magazine said that Coca had "the face of a junior gargoyle, the shape of a suspender strap."

Coca co-starred with Sid Caesar on the wildly popular Your Show of Shows in the 1950s, playing his wife and doing solo routines, including dances, songs, and pantomimes. In one routine, Coca played a model; and Caesar played a photographer who molded her features into whatever shape he wanted. Her ability to stretch her features to suit his "molding" underscored her image as the "woman with the rubber face." Said one critic: "Her face is a study of understated looniness....When the left side of her mouth curls upward and one eye sets off on an exploration of uncharted territory, when she arches her brows or bares her teeth, we know we are in the company of a clown in the glorious tradition of Beatrice Lillie."

In 1951, the Hearst newspaper chain named Coca the top comedienne in television. Her approach to humor, even slapstick, was subtler than Raye's and she had an airy, fey personality. Although some critics berated her for not looking like a glamour girl, others called her figure "slim and elfin" and pronounced her, "the cutest thing to ever hit the cabaret stage....she's so adorable you want to squeeze her till she pops."

Coca's off-beat appeal—Gawky Gertrude slapstick and mugging softened by her cute, pixyish persona—made her the perfect foil for Sid Caesar. She could match him in the broad comedy scenes while providing a feminine complement to his more aggressive comedy style.

The tendency of some critics to measure her against beauty contest standards says more about the media's tendency to stereotype women, especially performers, than it does about Coca, who was an attractive woman, albeit not a fashion model. No one took Sid Caesar to task for not looking as handsome as Gregory Peck or Montgomery Clift. But unrealistic, rigid standards of beauty have been consistently applied to female performers. The result? That actresses who could not meet these standards often fell back on comedy as a poor second choice. Once they discovered a gift for comedy, they often felt pressured to conform to a grotesque "type."

The two main types available to women were the dizzy dame or the homely slapsticker—usually an inept manchaser. Both these types afforded the female performer an avenue to express her talents and sometimes enabled her to amass considerable fame and fortune. However, the cost was often high. The women who played Dumb Doras and Gawky Gertrudes were often belittled by critics for their lack of either brains or good looks. Their cartoon-like personae expressed very little of the women's own complex personalities and talents. They over-emphasized their sex appeal, ugliness, dumbness, or boisterous aggression.

It's true that all comic characters are exaggerated, including those played by men. Male comics often play characters that are not particularly macho, but they have not had to deal with the notion that being funny in itself is somehow unmasculine. Comediennes have had to deal with a supposed conflict between femininity and funniness—unless their humor results from a kind of cute naiveté. Comediennes often experienced great frustration and insecurity. Gracie Allen even developed migraine headaches, and George Burns felt her problem was exacerbated by "the chronic strain of making like someone she isn't."

However, there have been some comediennes who did present themselves as consciously clever. These unusual women were and are able to succeed by asserting their intelligence—often along with their sexuality. Many of them write and perform their own material. Many, though not all, are stand-up comics—what Phyllis Diller calls the "hard core" of comedy, They fly solo, smart, and strong-minded. They are the wits and wisecrackers.

Sources

Ansen, David with Janet Huck, "The Great Goldie Rush," *Newsweek*, January 12, 1981, p.55.

Ball, Lucille, personal interview conducted at her home in New York, NY, April 14, 1984.

Behar, Joy, personal interview, conducted by telephone, 1993.

Behar, Joy, comedy act.

"Good ol' Grace," *Grace Under Fire*, ABC,1994.

Irwin, Rhoda, "Goldie," *Rolling Stone*, March 5, 1981, p.20.

"Joy Schtick" *New York*, November 9, 1992, p.51, 52.

Martin, Linda and Segrave, Kerry, *Women in Comedy* (Secaucus, New Jersey, Citadel Press, 1986) pp.157, 227, 114, 385, 55, 18, 214, 236, 252, 153

Playboy Interview: Goldie Hawn, *Playboy*, January 1985, p.87, 91.

The Adventures of Gracie, CBS Radio.

Wits and Wisecrackers

The Dumb Doras and Gawky Gertrudes entertain audiences by presenting images of women that are non-threatening—mentally limited, sexually neutered, or childish. They reflect fantasies about women—and only a fraction of women's real experience. No matter how brilliantly amusing, they are essentially objects of desire—or derision.

What happens when a woman presents herself not as object, but as subject? As not just desirable but as lustful—and not thereby ludricous, inept, or immoral? As not laughably ugly, but as laughing at rigid standards of beauty? As not mentally limited or silly, but as intelligent, with sometimes radical opinions? As fully conscious and fully human? Can she still be accepted? Can she still be funny?

The comic type that allows for conscious self-expression is the wit or wisecracker. She invites us to laugh not at her, but with her—often at some of our most cherished notions. She knows what's going on— and is articulate about what she thinks, feels, and wants. She is also apt to meet with a lot of resistance.

Historically, women were not supposed to be funny in the first place. The first American variety-type entertainments took place in "concert-saloons" and were designed to entertain a rowdy, male clientele. Women were a popular attraction at these saloons, not as performers but as waitresses. Their job was to serve drinks and flirt with the customers, often pocketing a percentage of the drinks they sold. Many of these "waitresses" were prostitutes. The concert-saloons and the women associated with them were popular with paying customers but scorned by respectable society. (Since the male customers came from all social stations, they were, of course, part of that society.)

By the 1850s, the entertainment included songs, dances, acrobatics, banjo playing, and crude comedy. To placate public opinion, the proprietors of these establishments removed the prostitutes (or at least kept them behind the scenes). To entice customers, women became part of the stage show—not as comics but as scantily clad chorus dancers. Their dances, which included the infamous can-can, were considered risqué and indecent—and, were of course, very enticing to the male clientele.

(Today's closest parallels are probably the topless bars, strip joints, and go-go clubs which feature titillating female entertainment. It is in establishments like these that many male comics [for example, Lenny Bruce, who was married to a stripper] and comediennes—including Totie Fields, Joan Rivers, and Goldie Hawn—got their start thirty or more years ago. The humor in most of these places was lewd and male-oriented, and the difficulty many of today's female comics have in establishing themselves can be traced back to the origin of stand-up comedy as part of crude saloon entertainment performed by men for a male clientele.)

In the 1860s the New York legislature passed a law prohibiting women from acting as waitresses in concert-saloons. Instead of using women to hustle drinks, saloon proprietors were forced to restrict the charms of their female employees to the stage. They changed the name of their establishments to "variety theatres" or "variety halls," and slowly women began to establish themselves as entertainers. Most female performers were still part of a briefly clad chorus line and expected to fraternize with the male customers. But a few were part of "man-woman" acts, with the man providing the comedy. (Many of the performing couples were married, which provided the wife with protection from the demands of the often lecherous male customers.)

An enterprising proprietor named Tony Pastor attempted to attract women customers by imposing a no-drinking, no-smoking policy, protecting female clients from "mashers" and cleaning up some of the off-color material. As other producers followed suit, the audience began to include more women—who liked to see material of interest to them, including domestic comedy.

By the 1890s the more gifted female performers in the "man-woman" acts were getting their share of laughs, and these variety shows were known as vaudeville. ("Vaudeville" is thought to be derived from "Val de Vire," the river valley in France with a tradition of bawdy songs.) Vaudeville, which was headquartered in New York, sent performers on tour all over the United States and had an enormous influence on the development of new talent, including many performers who went on to careers in film, radio, and television.

Besides the women who appeared in comedy/singing/dancing duos, there were a few solo female performers who did comedy. These unusual women did not present themselves as Dumb Doras or Gawky Gertrudes but as clever monologuists. One of the first was Beatrice Hereford, who portrayed a variety of comic characters in short pieces which she wrote herself. Hereford was appreciated by critics and fellow wits, including Dorothy Parker, who was an ardent fan. Another popular monologuist was Ruth Draper. Using a few props and elements of costume, Draper performed amusing playlets in imaginary settings, often involving other, invisible characters.

The story-like sketches of Hereford and Draper were part of a theatrical tradition which had included female performers since the European sixteenth century commedia dell'arte. Far more than stand-up comedy, which had its roots in the raucous variety halls of the nineteenth century and burst into bloom in the 1950s "Borsht Belt" (Catskill Mountain resort-hotels where the comics were almost exclusively male), sketch comedy and comedic plays, often with music or dancing, have been comparatively open to women. Until recently, a boy with show business ambitions and a flair for humor might well consider stand up comedy; a girl with similar aspirations and talents was far more likely to go into acting, singing, or dancing (especially if she were pretty). If she did go into comedy, it would most likely be as part of duo or ensemble, with only the exceptional woman braving the frontier of a solo act.

One of those who did was Sophie Tucker, who mixed music and humor. Tucker, born in 1884 and with a career that lasted through the 1960s, used a mixture of comedy patter and songs to put forward her own witty, sensual, philosophy of life. Instead of playing a dependent, Dumb Dora, or a sexually frustrated Gawky Gertrude, she portrayed herself as a strong individual—and a *successful* man-chaser.

For most of her career, Tucker was neither young nor svelte. But she advertised a sensuality as robust as a slim, glamour girl's and sang, "I've put a little more meat on. So what, there's more schmaltz (chicken fat) to sizzle when I turn the heat on!"

At two-hundred pounds, Tucker looked like a food-pushing/ consuming Jewish Mama. She underscored the maternal connection by singing a tear-wrenching version of "My Yiddisheh Mama," which regularly brought down the house.

(The idealized, immigrant mother was a popular type for many decades. Gertrude Berg, played a warm-hearted Jewish mother on the 1930s and 40s radio and television situation comedy, *The Goldbergs*, which she also wrote and produced. [The show was canceled in 1951 when Philip Loeb, who played Jake Goldberg, was blacklisted.] *I Remember Mama*, a 1950s television situation comedy based on the Broadway play of the same name, centered around a loving, strong Norwegian immigrant mother.)

However, despite Tucker's sentimental paean to the self-sacrificing, immigrant mother/homemaker, the singer herself (born while her parents were en route to America) rejected the restrictions of marriage and motherhood to carve out an independent career that lasted for sixty years. By age thirteen (and 145 pounds), she was helping support her family by singing in amateur contests. To get away from home and give vent to her own lusty nature, she married at a local boy, Louis Tuck, at sixteen without parental consent. Then, pregnant and desperate to escape the poverty that had entrapped her own mother, she left the baby with her parents and set out to seek her fortune in show business.

Considered too fat and homely to sing as a white woman, Tucker sang "coon melodies" in blackface,but made her mark as a Jewish comedienne by mixing the maternal with the sexual, billing herself as a "red-hot mama," and kidding sex. She mocked both Jewish and Gentile concepts of feminine modesty, and belted out ribald plaints (mainly by Fred Fish, her favorite songwriter) against her ice-cold papa and the general unreliability of men.

One of her most popular songs by Fish went: "Mistah Siegal, you better make it legal" and reduced the tragedy of a seduced and abandoned woman to a pathetic-funny plight of a Jewish girl trying to get the no-goodnik who who put a *kiegle* (noodle pudding) in her belly to marry her. Instead of Hester Prynne's Scarlet Letter, we have a pregnant *schlimazl's* (luckless fool)'s *kiegle.*

In another song, a pregnant secretary demands payment for services rendered, "When am I getting my mink, Mr. Fink?" Instead of a shamefaced, fallen woman, we have a brassy employee demanding fair wages from her "cheapskate" boss. And from the Yiddish tradition, we have the *schnorrer* (beggar)—who demands her due ("look at all the room rent I saved you in the back seat of your automobile!") with wit and *chutzpah* (nerve).

Unlike Fanny Brice, whose signature song "My Man" proclaimed her undying devotion to a faithless man, Tucker's songs and comic advice declared her emotional independence from the vagaries of romance. If a man strayed, she advised women to face facts: "No One Woman Can Satisfy Any One Man All the Time," dry her tears, and "get yourself a filler-inner."

She further advised her audience to enjoy sensuality without apology, proclaiming: "You've Got to Be Loved to Be Healthy." Nor was marriage necessary for a fully satisfying life. Long before the modern women's liberation movement, Tucker sang her own declaration of independence: "I'm Living Alone and I Like It."

In her own life, Tucker, who was married and divorced three times, felt her hard-won independence cost her some romantic appeal "Once you start carrying your own suitcases, paying your own bills, running your own show, you've done something to yourself that makes you one of those women men may like and call a pal and a good sport, the sort of woman they tell their troubles to. But you've cut yourself off from the orchids and diamond bracelets, except those you buy yourself." Whether the homely, two-hundred pound, middle-aged Tucker would have gotten orchids and diamonds *without* a successful entertainment career is certainly open to speculation. In any case, fat, feisty, and fifty- plus, Tucker continued delighting audiences with a droll, robust attitude toward sensuality until 1966 when she died at the age of seventy nine.

Mae West, Tucker's slightly younger contemporary, also played the role of the strong, smart, sensual woman. Born in 1892, Mae West began in vaudeville in 1914 and wrote her own starring vehicle *Diamond Lil* for the Broadway stage in the 1920s. She transferred her basic character—a swaggering, diamond-sporting, tongue-in-cheek sex goddess—to her 1930s comedy films, wrote her own slyly suggestive dialogue, and became the highest paid entertainer in the country.

West was forty when she made her first film, with a matronly figure that was fully covered in period costumes from the 1890s. Although not as fat as Tucker, her figure was hefty; and her sexuality was also primarily verbal and based on innuendo—not direct physical display. Some of her most famous lines have become classics of innuendo.

Between two evils, I always pick the one I never tried before.

Do you have a gun in your pocket...or are you just glad to see me?

And of course:

Come up and see me sometime…(The original version, spoken to Cary Grant in the film She Done Him Wrong, was "Why don't you come sometime and see me? I'm home every evening. Come up. I'll tell your fortune.")

Like Tucker, West's relations with other female characters were sisterly and helpful (unless crossed by a snobbish, so-called "respectable" women who patronized her manners or morals). She comforts a tearful girl who had been seduced and abandoned with a salty observation: "When girls go wrong, men go right after them." Both Tucker and West flaunted a level of sexuality and aggression that was softened by their age, matronly appearance and good humor. (Moms Mabley, a black comedienne whose act was even more bawdy, presented an even less sexy, motherly appearance. Dr. Ruth Westheimer, a contemporary sex therapist and entertaining media personality, operates in much the same mode. Her enthusiastic, even graphic references to sexuality are tempered by her matronly appearance, friendly attitude, and humor.)

Despite all her innuendoes, West was not a sex object like Marilyn Monroe, who portrayed herself as the vulnerable object of men's desires. West was the driving force of her own life, which included an active libido, and once remarked, "I am the woman's ego."

Much of the appeal of Tucker and West was based on their daring, amusing suggestiveness in an era in which women who were ladies never alluded to sex in public. They were able to both rebel against the propriety of their era and be protected by it. In today's more permissive climate, the public expression of sexuality and aggression is more blatant. It's harder to titillate an audience with amusingly suggestive material when they have just been exposed to graphic references, often couched in obscene language.

One of the first women comics to use really blue material was Belle Barth, (born Belle Salzman), who began performing in the 1920s and 1930s, mixing jokes with bawdy songs. If Sophie Tucker and Mae West were slyly suggestive; Barth was graphic—(she was labeled the "female Lenny Bruce"). She was also the first woman to use a format of short jokes—usually dirty. Male comics had, of course, been telling dirty jokes for years. What made Barth's act special was not only that, as a woman, she spoke about matters and used language normally considered a male preserve, but that her graphic material came from a woman's point of view. Instead of women as object, she was subject—laughing at the inadequacies and delusions of the male ego.

For example, she quipped that, "The most difficult thing for a woman to do on the first night of her second marriage is to holler it hurts!" and for her husband "to tie his feet to the bed so he doesn't fall in and drown!"

Barth found an audience for her blue humor in nightclubs and hotels and made a number of party records including, *If I Embarrass You, Tell Your Friends.* Unlike Tucker and West, she never achieved a mass following. A woman performing raunchy material was shocking and unacceptable to many of her contemporaries and limited her to the club circuit. However, she was a trailblazer for some of today's women comics, like Roseanne, who now have license to use direct sexual and scatological references, Nevertheless, with some exceptions, female comics still rarely say anything approaching the pornographic material of some of the dirty male comics. Like most women, most comediennes, whether due to personal inclination or a sense of what is socially acceptable, are simply not as crude as male comics.

A bawdy contemporary of Belle Barth was the Afro-American comedienne Jackie "Moms" Mabley.

> Jack was my first boyfriend. I was real uptight with him and he was real uptight with me....He took a lot off me and the least I could do was take his name.

Mabley began her career in the 1920s and performed through the 1970s. Mabley, who started performing in her early twenties, quickly adopted the stage character of "Moms," a salty granny who sang, danced, and told stories—often raunchy. In her early years, segregation forced her to confine her early performances to the Negro "chitlin circuit," (which white comics used to visit—often to steal her material).

> I don't care if you could stand on your eyebrows. If you was colored, you couldn't get no work, nohow.

As racial restrictions loosened in the 1960s, she was able to offer her brand of spicy humor to large, racially mixed audiences. Many of her routines were based on portraying herself as a "dirty old woman" with an eye for young men:

> The only thing an old man can do for me is to bring me a note from a young man.

Some of her later routines involved her giving advice to world leaders, like President Lyndon Johnson. Her phonograph records were extremely popular. Her first album *Moms Mabley, The Funniest*

Woman in the World, sold over a million copies. In 1966, she recorded a second album *Now Hear This,* with humor so raunchy it was regularly played at stag parties.

Where Mabley built her career on one character, "Moms," Lily Tomlin plays a wide variety of characters, usually in short monologues, sometimes in dialogue with other invisible characters. Her sketches owe much to Ruth Draper; and in fact Tomlin used to listen to Ruth Draper's phonograph records over and over.

Tomlin came to national attention in 1969 doing sketch comedy on *Laugh-In.* One of her most popular characters was Ernestine, the smug telephone operator with a snorting laugh, and a habit of inquiring "Is this the party to whom I'm speaking?" Another was Edith Ann, a precocious five-year-old who sits in a big rocker and muses "Sometimes I like to sit on the drain in the bathtub when the water's running out. It feels so inneresting." Edith Ann also offers philosophical tidbits like "When I'm happy I feel like crying, but when I'm sad, I don't feel like laughing. I think it's better to be happy. Then you get two feelings for the price of one." Says Tomlin:

Here's what set me apart and gave me a lot of breaks. I created specific characters and specific monologues to convey specific things, because I was always mostly interested in commenting on the culture.

Soon after her *Laugh-In* success, Tomlin teamed up with writer/director Jane Wagner, and together the team have created record albums, television specials, movies, two Broadway shows, and hundreds of characters. Among them are: Tommy Velour, the quintessential male lounge singer, with unbuttoned shirt, gold chains, and a hairy chest, Lupe, the World's Oldest Beauty expert, the Rubber Freak, Suzy Sorority of the Silent Majority, and even a reporter who "interviews" Tomlin, leading her to confess that despite her normal appearance, she has starred in a shocking film about heterosexuality—even playing a frankly heterosexual women. "People just don't understand," sighs Lily, "You don't have to be one to play one."

Their most successful venture was the one-woman Broadway show *The Search for Signs of Intelligent Life in the Universe,* with characters like Trudy, the bag lady, whose shock treatments have left her with a direct line to aliens from outer space who confide that they have come here "to look at a planet in puberty" and that "reality is nothing but a collective hunch." Asked to comment on the impact of the Woman's Movement on her career, Tomlin said dryly: "If it weren't for the Women's Movement, people would call it my hobby."

Tomlin has never performed stand-up comedy. In that, she is typical of many female performers, who appear in sketches, plays, and films or combine singing with comedy. One of the best known singer/actress/comediennes is Bette Midler, who turned her unconventional looks into her own brand of fabulous sex-cum-comic appeal. Midler started out as a singer, but her career didn't really take off until she began performing a mixture of singing and bawdy comedy to a male homosexual audience at the Continental Baths, where Midler introduced herself as, "The Divine Miss M—everything you were afraid your little girl would grow up to be…and your little boy." Midler's ribald commentary often focused on her own ample anatomy. She once confessed that she used a postage scale to figure out how heavy her breasts were:

> I won't tell you how much they weigh, but it cost $87.50 to ship them to Brazil. Third Class.

Stints on Johnny Carson's *The Tonight Show* followed, and Midler was soon touring the country with an act that mingled singing and comedy. She delivered her "dirty Sophie Tucker jokes" in the character of "Soph," an old woman with an outsized libido. (Like Moms Mabley, Midler discovered that raunchy material was better accepted in the character of an old woman; and that she was able to defy her own ladylike upbringing when in character as "Soph" or the "Divine Miss M.") Midler made the transition to films, winning an Academy Award nomination for her portrayal of Janis Joplin in The Rose, based on the doomed life of the rock star. After a few flops, Midler hit her stride with three comedies, which were in the top ten at the box office: *Down and Out in Beverly Hills, Outrageous Fortune, Ruthless People,* and *Big Business.* She went on to play Woody Allen's wife in *Scenes from a Mall,* a witch in *Hocus Pocus,* and the Martha Raye role in *For the Boys.* An outsized talent who can sing, dance, and play both comedy and drama, Midler is under utilized in an era that makes very few "women's pictures—or musicals. However, she is philosophical:

> I know I'm lucky to be where I am, because then I would never have made the cut. I don't have the face for it, and I don't have the body. I don't have anything they required except the enthusiasm and the drive.

Like Midler, Whoopi Goldberg, (born Karyn Johnson in a New York City Housing project) an Afro-American comedienne/actress, is not conventionally pretty. And, again like Midler, she made her initial fame with a solo act that spotlighted her unusual talents. She developed an hour long one-woman show called The Spook Show, showcasing four original characters. She toured the show in the United States and Europe, finally opening in 1984 on Broadway as

Whoopi Goldberg. Like Lily Tomlin, she played a variety of characters, including a child and a handicapped person. (Earlier, she had portrayed Mabley in *MOMS,* a show based on the life of Moms Mabley.) But where Tomlin's characters are often fey/philosophical, Whoopi's personae often have a raw, painful subtext, and slip between comedy, pathos, and anger.

Goldberg opens the show as "Fontaine," an educated male junkie who steals gold-plated, digital escargot forks and counsels a self-righteous male "pro-life" demonstrator: ("I have the answer to abortion—shoot your dick!") Fontaine intimidates an airline stewardess ("I looked in your wallet, and I know where you live") into putting him on the first flight for Amsterdam. There, he visits the Anne Frank house and experiences an epiphany about the need to move beyond prejudice and selfishness into compassion. For the remainder of the rest of the show, Whoopi crosses lines of race, age, and physical normalcy to play a white thirteen-year-old Surfer Girl whose self-induced abortion causes permanent sterility; a five-year-old black child who pretends to be white by wearing a shirt on her head to simulate her "long, luxurious, blond hair"; and a cripple who achieves bird-like grace in her dreams.

Steven Spielberg saw her in the show and cast her in *The Color Purple,* where she had her first on screen kiss—with another woman. She has gone on to star in several feature films including *Jumpin' Jack Flash, Burglar, Fatal Beauty. Clara's Heart, The Telephone, Homer, and Edie, Ghost, The Long Walk Home, Soapdish, Sarafina! Sister Act,* and *Sister Act II.* The fact that Goldberg has been able to star in a Broadway show and numerous feature films as well as host a television talk show reflects her talent, determination and the loosening of old restrictions of sex and race. Goldberg states:

> I don't talk about myself as a woman. I don't talk about myself as being black. Because for other people that's a problem. I didn't do anything, and I've been real clear with everybody that woman or not, there's nothing they're gonna keep me from doing.

In the same way, today's exploding numbers of female stand-up comics challenge ideas about women not being funny or assertive enough to make it in a traditionally masculine profession. So ingrained were those ideas that it wasn't until the 1960s that female comics like Totie Fields, Phyllis Diller, and Joan Rivers carved big-time careers as stand-up acts. To get past resistance, they used what we now call "self-deprecating humor" mainly about their lack of sex appeal, and played to the notion "She's not pretty, so she has to be funny."

Totie Fields was born Sophie Feldman. "Totie" came from her childhood pronunciation of her first name; and "Feldman" was shortened to "Fields." She started out as a singer and idolized Sophie Tucker, who came backstage and advised the young Fields to take every penny she had and put it into her stage wardrobe. Fields followed the advice, and the next time Tucker saw her, she said "Perfect."

Like Tucker, Fields, who was four foot ten inches and weighed over 170 pounds, made mirth out of her girth. Turning around to display a size 18 dress that looked like a sequined tent, she would demand:

How do you like the new dress? I look like a pregnant snowball, huh?

Actually, I'm losing a lot of weight lately. (pointing to the folds of flab under her arms) Look how everything hangs on me.

She was good-naturedly willing to present herself as a fat sex symbol—singing "Sexy Me" ("You're gonna see cheeks, lips, and hips like you've never seen before") while bemoaning the discomfort of obesity ("Do you know how hard it is to be sexy when your feet are coming over the sides of your shoes.") Strutting in front of a male ringsider, she cooed, "You're dying to touch me, aren't you, ya animal!...Ooh! look! He can't keep his eyes off me...." The men in the audience roared with laughter, and she rewarded them by pasting gold stars on their foreheads.

Fields' mixed-message: that it was ridiculous to think of her as sexy, but that (thanks to perfect grooming, a fancy wardrobe, good-humored sensuality, and abundant curves), she somehow was appealing disarmed the men and created a bond with women. Said Fields:

I actually did wear a size 9 once, but I was about half as tall, so I was still the same build. And so what? That's the key to my act; most of the world isn't built like Elizabeth Taylor. They see I can laugh at myself and that gives them reassurance, new confidence.

Fields' ability to relate to the average woman came out of her own homelife. Married to bandleader/manager George Johnston, she had two daughters. When they left home, she used the "empty-nest" experience as material for her act.

I'm doing a thing about my kids right now, and every word is true. How the kids left the house, and I've never been happier in my life. The first week you're miserable and miss them, but by the second week you're walking around the house naked again, and it's fun. And every woman in the audience screams.

At the peak of her popularity, Fields earned $200,000 a year. She credits Phyllis Diller with breaking down the financial ceiling for women comics.

> For a long time I got twice the laughs of a mediocre comic for the same money. I always give credit to Phyllis Diller. She was the first really big female comic in this country. When they couldn't afford Phyllis, they said, "What else you got in a comedienne? And there I was. Phyllis is the reason I got a chance. And I think Joanie Rivers should thank me—I think I opened the door for her. That the way it works—each person helps the others.

And, in a moment of philosophic introspection:

There was discrimination, yes, but what are you going to do? Cry about it or go out and beat it down....The only thing I ever wanted when I was playing those $75-a-week toilets was that I shouldn't become envious of others. I try to keep envy and bitterness out of my system. I think you're funnier when you do.

In her late forties, complications following minor cosmetic surgery led to phlebitis. the amputation of her leg, and early death. Even after the amputation, she gamely continuing to perform, joking: "At least, I have a leg to stand on."

Like Fields, Diller and Rivers make jokes about their unappealing bodies. Diller dresses in balloon-like costumes to hide her slim figure; Rivers verbally abuses herself despite an attractive appearance. They are Gawky Gertrudes as wisecrackers. Fields, Diller, and Rivers found that self-deprecating humor helped them open the door to acceptance. As Diller puts it, "It endears you to the audience....If some of the girls did it, they would get ahead further and faster."

In 1976, psychologist Joan Levine reported that according to her research:

> Females indulge in self-deprecatory humor to a greater extent than do males....the data showed that women deprecated themselves 63 percent of the time; males railed against their own individual shortcomings in a total of 12 percent of their cuts. The men may make more jibes against their gender, but not at their own expense....Unless more research reveals a different etiology for the genesis of self-deprecatory humor, it can be surmised that comediennes are echoing the values of their social milieu in order to attract and keep a mass audience.

Some of this is changing, as a new style of assertive, even aggressive women's comedy emerged in the 1970s. This style, strongly impacted by the women's liberation movement, focuses on the oppressiveness of the patriarchal culture, not on the inadequacy of the individual woman comic. However, old styles and ways of feeling and thinking don't change overnight. Many women comics still infuse their comedy with self-deprecation—a style of humor often shared by other oppressed groups.

Psychologist Samuel Janus has written about self-belittling humor as a dominant strain among Jews, who use it as a "defense mechanism to ward off the aggression and hostility of others....Though self-deprecation is traditional in Jewish humor, it has a special function in America: it serves as a ritual exorcism for conflicts shared with Jewish audiences, and it assures Gentile audiences that Jewish humor is not threatening."

The same holds true with traditional African-American comic types. Stepin Fetchit, (born Lincoln Theodore Monroe Andrew Perry in 1902), survived in vaudeville and films by presenting himself as amusingly slow-witted, superstitious, and timid. Amos & Andy, a compendium of ludicrous, racial stereotypes, began on the radio as the creations of white writers and actors. When the show aired on television, and the actors could be seen as well as heard, it was necessary to hire blacks to play the roles. The black actors simply continued playing the characters as originally conceived. It wasn't until the advent of the civil rights movement that assertive black comedians of the 1960s like Dick Gregory, Richard Pryor, and Bill Cosby portrayed their insider's humorous, sometimes angry view of the black experience to mixed audiences.

And it wasn't until the 1970s that the women's movement gave an impetus to female performers to crack the near monopoly men had on stand-up comedy or to use their comedy to challenge the sexist assumptions behind most stand-up material."You didn't really see women break out in comedy until the feminist movement made it possible for women to be considered funny without degrading themselves." explains Caroline Hirsch, founder of Caroline's Comedy Club in New York.

Why has there been so much resistance to female stand-up comics? Joy Behar, a headlining comic with her own radio and television show explains:

> Comedy is a powerful position. You're up there (on stage) all alone. We're not raised to be funnier than the boys or be in a more powerful position than men. It goes against the social order of things. In that sense, it's harder for women.

Sociological studies show that in mixed-sex conversations, men tend to initiate topics, interrupt, and despite the stereotype about talkative women, just plain talk more. Robin Tyler, a feminist-activist comic, says, "Men are used to having women be the reactors, to listening. When the female comic has the mike, the men have to listen."

What's more, the driving force behind the funny words is often anger. Says Behar, "Comedians are angry. We need comedy to defend ourselves against the cruel world. But anger is great. It gives you an edge." One reason that there may be fewer women comics is that men are usually more comfortable expressing anger and taking an aggressive stance; and overt anger and aggression are less socially acceptable in women. Tyler comments, "Stand-up comedy is the eternal battle between comic and audience. Women are not supposed to do that with a man, let alone a whole audience."

Perhaps the reason that there is more resistance to women in stand-up comedy more than in say, sketch comedy or comedy films or plays, is that stand-up is experienced as a power struggle—one against the crowd. The performer directly dominates, or is dominated by an adversarial audience. Cynthia Coe, former director of artists management at New York's Catch a Rising Star comedy club comments, "Stand-up comedy is an inherently aggressive and potentially hostile art form....Even the language is violent. If you do well, you 'kill,' and if not, you bomb."

The most resistant audiences—for both male and female comics—are male, mainly because they equate laughter with losing control. Comic Jerry Seinfeld says: "It's easier with women; they're more open. I've always felt an audience dominated by women is great for me because they don't have any withholds on getting silly and doing things for fun. A woman's sense of humor is much more free, open, and loving—it doesn't even have to make sense. If it's fun, great."

Even if the women in the audience think the performer is funny, they may repress their laughter to conform to the reactions of the men. Comic Sandra Shamus recalls:

> Last time I did my show, there was a table right in front with a man in the middle and a woman on each side. The women were laughing and just giving it up! They were grabbing the table and it was like their lungs were coming out of their mouths! The man? Nothing. Then the women would look at him and stop laughing...until they connected again with me.

Besides the audience's discomfort with laughing at a woman comic, comediennes often have to contend with blatant hostility on the part of some male comics and m.c.'s. The "dick jokes" that are standard fare in most comedy clubs exclude women, who can't joke about their "dicks." Many of these jokes denigrate women as vulnerable and despicable sex objects. Comic Margaret Smith recalls the m.c. who introduced her by saying, "I like to fuck women with no legs. That way I can put them on my dick and spin them around. And now, here's Margaret Smith."

Both male and female comics have to deal with hecklers. This is apt to be particularly difficult for women. Many men are socialized to tease and banter with their buddies in a way that most women find personally insulting. Many men are also socialized to publicly express aggression and sexuality in a way that most women find intimidating or crude. Heckling in a comedy club is an intensified version of insult humor that many men are accustomed to dishing out—and handling. What makes it even more threatening is the fact that heckling frequently takes the form of denigrating the female performer as a sex object. In order to successfully handle hecklers, a female comic has to set aside the wounds to her feminine ego, overcome her socialization as a lady, and take charge of the situation—subtly or aggressively.

When comic Paula Poundstone mused that "professional sports don't do a thing for me," a male heckler demanded, "What does?" Poundstone replied, "Of course I enjoy you very, very much. Beyond that? Well, I watch a lot of movies..." When the heckler insinuated "What kind?" Poundstone sighed, "I see you're determined to go in that direction. Let's nip that in the bud, right now, shall we?"

Less courteous comediennes fight fire with fire, and resort to the sexual put-downs that are standard fare in most comic clubs: "How about taking your hand off your wee-wee and listening?" Or: "Oh look! A penis—only smaller!"

Some comediennes have even adopted a male style of attack humor. "Pudgie," billed as the female Don Rickles, picks on members of her audience as the butts of her brand of insult humor. Sandra Bernhard mix 'n matches seduction and sadism as she stalks a male audience member with routines like: "Phil, you are taking a fashion risk and it's working. I really like you. I'm attracted to you. And yet"—she narrows her eyes and hisses—"there is something about you that makes me want to hurt you. I'd really like to smash your face."

What caused the change from self-deprecation to self-assertion and aggression? Caroline Hirsch sees Elaine Boosler, who broke through in the feminist mid-1970s and is one of today's leading comics, as a pioneer for the new style of women's comedy. Says Hirsch:

She was one of the first women to open it up. Not only was her timing right with the comedy boom and changing attitudes in society; she is also brilliant. Elayne has certain standards about women's issues and about the business that have definitely hurt her. It is still a man's world, but she refuses to play games.

Comedian Richard Lewis comments:

At that time, there was, like an irrational belief among most male comics that it was their "turf." Elayne really cracked a hole into that consciousness. She was the Jackie Robinson of my generation. She was the strongest female working. She broke the mold for female comics.

Says comic Jay Leno:

If someone challenges Elayne's femininity, she doesn't back off two steps and become coy. She is to female comedy what Dick Gregory and Richard Pryor are to black comedy.

In fact, Boosler's humor eschews jokes about her supposed fat thighs or trouble getting a man. She takes a sharp-eyed look at the icons of society, including the Vatican:

The Vatican came down with a new ruling. They said no surrogate mothers.... A good thing they didn't make this rule before Jesus was born!

She also skewers media hypocrisy:

Don't you think it's awful that networks won't advertise condoms because of pressure from religious groups? Wouldn't it be wonderful if we found out you can only get AIDS by giving money to television preachers?

Even when Boosler does body jokes, it's to poke fun at women's self-deprecation ("every woman in the world thinks her behind is too big") rather than belittling her own anatomy. When she does a PMS jokes, it's as a sign of female power. Imagining herself as the first female president, she intimidates a terrorist:

Taking hostages on a day when I'm retaining water? This is going to go very badly for you!

Boosler dismisses the idea that she is a militant feminist:

When asked if I'm a feminist, I've always said that I'm just a human being trapped in a woman's body.

But while many of her comic peers were scrambling up the show business ladder, Boosler often found herself stepping on a loose rung.

I went in to do the *Tonight* show. I had a beautiful set all prepared, and they put someone on my case to write the jokes. I remember the first joke I was handed went "I'm so ugly, I can't make a nickel on a battleship." I just refused to do it.

In time, Boosler's brand of non-sexist comedy has found its audience—she has a cable television special, regularly headlines around the country, and is writing screenplays.

Other women comics who were shaped by the social movements of the 1960s and 1970s are veteran performers Adrienne Tolsch and Emily Levine. Adrienne Tolsch talks about the problem of male resistance to female-oriented material:

The trouble is, there's no "guy stuff." There's "stuff" and then there's "woman stuff," and some guys don't want to hear it. They think you're going to get disgusting because it's new to them. But if they'll listen, and that's all I ask, they'll inevitably come around.

Tolsch's material used to focus on the male/female relationships, and much of it was painfully funny. Twice divorced, she recalled:

When I was married, my husband would wake me in the middle of the night to perform. So if any time during my act I roll over and say "Not tonight," please understand.

When she was single she joked about dating problems of female comics:

Dating is not easy when you get off work at 4 a.m. like I do. You know who's up at that hour? Guys in Europe.

Now married to Bill Scheft, a fellow stand-up comic and staff writer on the David Letterman show, Tolsch does more family-oriented material. In one of her routines, she imagines her aunt working as a 900 phone sex operator. "So what are you wearing?" whines the aunt in a voice that would slice lunch meat. The terrified client mumbles "Everything I've ever owned...As a matter of fact, I'm putting things on as we speak."

Emily Levine started in comedy in the 1970s as the only female member of an improvisational group called *The New York City Stickball Team*. The group became an instant hit and attracted a star-studded audience of older male comics. Levine recalls the night Milton Berle, Jan Murray, and David Fry came backstage to celebrate.

We would all be standing there, and these guys would come up to me and put their arm around me like I was some sort of prop and say, "Hey, you guys were great." And then they'd look at me and say, "Oh, and you were real cute, honey." It was so humiliating. I can't describe it, and you couldn't explain it to any of those men. They hadn't done anything patently offensive. It was just that I was "the girl."

Soon after, Levine wrote a one-woman show for herself, and gradually evolved into stand-up comedy—often with feminist overtones.

> Every time I go to a mechanic, they treat me like I'm stupid. I know what a gasket is. A gasket is $150. But a "gasket-honey" is $200.

Levine says, "Most of the 'woman stuff' I do is in respect to sexual politics. I find the other stuff difficult to talk about, not always so much for me, but in terms of audience reaction." Like many other female comics, Levine was heckled about her lack of sex appeal. When a male audience member yelled, "you remind me of my mother!" Radcliffe graduate Levine shot back: "Why? Did your mother go to Harvard too?"

If Tolsch, Behar, and Levine are sharp-tongued wisecrackers, Lotus Weinstock's is a softer cookie—but with bite. Weinstock first developed her act in the early 1960s, but it didn't catch on: "Somehow the audience had a hard time accepting hip humor from a woman in pumps and beehive." Working with a male partner, she played a Dumb Dora—a cross between Gracie Allen and Marilyn Monroe:

> I was into cleavage consciousness—a look that made me seem like I didn't have much upstairs. Marilyn Monroe was my fashion guru— my hair was maybe a touch too blond, a little too much cleavage showing. I was doing heady things, but I looked sexy. When I had my male partner, it was perfect because he was there. I looked like I was the victim. We were like the Smothers Brothers—I was the dumber but shrewder one. I would say things like I didn't know what I was saying, but I was getting zingers in there. I was a wide-eyed, dead-pan, cleavaged, powdered, perfumed thing. He was there to comment for the audience. When I moved out on my own, I noticed that whenever I said things that involved one or two thoughts it was hard for people. It conflicted with the way I looked. The real conflict was in me— how I felt about myself.

Weinstock went out to California and became a flower child ("Lotus" is courtesy of a 1960s commune). She also met Lenny Bruce, to whom she was engaged when he died of a drug overdose in 1966. Says Weinstock, "He was like a prophet, a seeker. He knew comedy had to have substance, and he busted me on all my little phony tricks."

Today Weinstock, who tucks a flower behind one ear, performs comedy that plays against her persona as a "Dumb Dora." Spoofing an article advising women to use seductive body language, her words and gestures mock the patronizing advice, as her flowing, pastel garments and fluffy blonde hair underscore her own femininity. One night, a male heckler interrupted her explanation of a marriage manual, ("First the man...") by asking, "Do I do this with a man?" "No." replied Weinstock. "This is pro-choice." Then, turning to the rest of the audience with spaniel eyes, she cooed, "I came back pretty quick, didn't I?"

Like Weinstock, Pam Stone, a slender blonde with a southern accent, plays off her own femininity and talks about the over-delicacy of southern belles.

> I'm not much of a Southern belle. Southern women tend to be real demure. They don't like to talk about anything graphic. I had a girlfriend who told me she was in the hospital for *female* problems. I said, "Get real! What does that mean?" She says, "You know, female problems." I said, "What? You can't parallel park? You can't get credit?"

Standing on tippytoes to be kissed, while girlishly swinging one foot up in the air, Stone muses about prehistoric female instincts ("while we're kissing the guy, we're kicking ourselves for getting involved").

Jenny Jones, another pretty blonde, mocks male seduction ploys;

> If you want to seduce a woman, invite her over and cook for her. Afterwards, she'll sit on a couch and say, "I want to show you how much I appreciate that wonderful dinner...I love macaroni and cheese...I just never had to slice it before....oh, maybe a metal knife and fork would be better...it's just so romantic eating over the sink. More? Oh, don't open a can just for me."

She also pokes fun at male sexual insecurity and the double standard:

> You guys who went to Catholic school need to loosen up. This one guy said to me, "Am I the first one?" I said, "Yeah. Today."

Another variation of not-so-Dumb Dora is Rita Rudner, whose waiflike prettiness and spacey logic evoke the young Gracie Allen. Rudner delivers her subtle, clever zingers with a wistful innocence that belie the hard work behind her craft. A former dancer, Rudner decided that comedy put her more in control of her own destiny. "I wanted to do something by myself. I didn't have to wait for someone to write it. I didn't have to wait for someone to hire me."

To prepare for her new profession, she applied the discipline of her ballet training and spent years studying comedy, watching clips of

George Burns, Jack Benny, and Woody Allen. "Listening to Woody Allen, all of a sudden, I realized that you didn't have to be aggressive.... My humor is more off-beat hysterical than it is raucous."

Like Allen, Rudner portrays herself as a sensitive loser. She explains why she and her former boyfriend broke up:

> He wanted to get married, and I didn't want him to.

Determined to find a suitable husband, she reasons airily:

> I like men with pierced ears. They're better prepared for marriage. They've experienced pain and bought jewelry.

She is now married to producer Martin Bergman, who coached her on how to package herself as an entertainment product, instructing her on how to give interviews, her onstage wardrobe, publicity campaigns,etc. She now headlines in theatres and large casinos, and the couple has co-written a film *Peter's Friends,* where she plays a neurotic actress. However, despite her career and marital success, Rudner still finds ways to build touches of her sexual loser persona into her act:

> My husband complained that I wore baggy clothes. I showed him. I wore spandex—he wouldn't touch me for a month.

Like Rivers, (who also continued her sexual loser persona after marriage), Rudner obsesses about her weight—but with a fey twist.

> I weigh myself holding on to the shower curtain rod. When I reach the weight I want, I black out.

But unlike hard-headed Rivers, and despite her own clear-headed practicality, Rudner professes a "feminine" confusion about money.

> I knew so little about money, I used to sign my checks, "Love, Rita."

If today's not-so-dumb Doras play with and against their own type, so do today's Gawky Gertrudes. But where Gawky Gertrude types used to downgrade their attractiveness for laughs, today's comediennes challenge media stereotypes of feminine appeal.

Today's best known version of Gawky Gertrude is Roseanne. Like Totie Fields, Roseanne's full-sized figure does not conform to fashion norms. But then, conformity has never been her strong suit.

Roseanne (born Barr, formerly Arnold) grew up Jewish in Mormon Salt Lake City. An automobile accident at age sixteen resulted in a trauma that landed her in a mental institution for eight months.

When she got out, she journeyed west, where she met and married her first husband, Bill Pentland, had three children, and lived in a trailer. Her younger sisters introduced her to a woman's bookstore, where she read feminist literature for two years. She spent a brief stint as a cocktail waitress, where she would insult customers with remarks like "Those drinks are gonna be six bucks, and it'll cost you three more to have me take 'em off the tray and put 'em on the table." Customers laughed, and soon were coming in just to be insulted. Roseanne decided to become a stand-up comic, basing her act on her own life as a working class wife and mother. She dubbed herself a "domestic goddess," (spoofing a right-wing best-seller called *Fascinating Womanhood*, that urged women to fulfill themselves in domestic submission). Her proletarian feminism brought her headliner status, an HBO special, and her own situation comedy, based around her life.

Rude, crude, and fat, Roseanne is everything a woman is not supposed to be. Totie Fields mocked her girth with self-deprecatory humor. But Roseanne flaunts her figure and opinions:"fat is comforting and sexy...Being fat, for a woman, also means you take up more space."

> I realized I had to create a whole new kind of comedy called "funny womanness," But there wasn't any language to name women's experience and make it funny to men and women....I felt I had to invent the language. So we're sitting there thinking, me and my husband and my sisters, and I go, "Oh my God! I've got it! The language is my life! Because I am a housewife! I'm not gonna go outside myself and say what I should be, I'm gonna say what is." And I suddenly knew that I could do what Richard Pryor did for himself—get inside the stereotype and make it three-dimensional from within. And then I could call myself a domestic goddess. Then I could say, "Hey fellas, you've had it wrong all these years, we women are not the funny ones, we women are not the jokes. You are the jokes!"

Zapping home her jokes with buzz saw sarcasm, Roseanne slices through sentimental sops to marriage and motherhood.

> My husband walks in the door one night, he says to me "Roseanne, don't you think it's time we sat down and had a serious talk about our sex life?" I say to him, "You want me to turn off *Wheel of Fortune* for that?"

> I figure when my husband comes home from work, if the kids are still alive, then I've done my job.

As for male sexual superiority, Roseanne responds with Belle Barth bluntness:

> Guys are pissed off at women because we know they only want one thing. That one thing ain't even in our top ten, and we still like it better than they do!

If naive Lucy Ricardo was a sitcom domestic goddess for the 1950s—then cynical Roseanne Conner, (Roseanne's sitcom alter-ego) is one for the 1990s. Despite differences in style, both shows affirm family values. Manners have changed; mores have changed (Roseanne accompanies her tv teenage daughter to the doctor's office to get birth control). But core values have not. The family stays together, and like Lucy and Ricky, Roseanne and television husband Dan (John Goodman) are in love.

Family values come under fire when a spouse is abusive—the off-screen history behind *Grace Under Fire,* a situation comedy based on the life of its star, Brett Butler, a survivor of domestic abuse. Butler escaped a disastrous first marriage to a bad ol' boy who beat her every day, and honed her persona—blue-collar, Southern broad who shoots from the lip—on the stand up comedy circuit. Carsey-Werner, the same production house that created *Roseanne,* distilled her act into a sitcom about an oil refinery worker and single mom, and propelled its proletarian heroine into Nielsen's 1993 top ten after only two episodes.

Butler's tv alter ego Grace Kelly ("like the actress except I'm a better driver") gets by on Southern sass and spunk. No alimony. No child support. No sex life. ("I don't even have time to put the shower head on pulse.")

And no time for feminist nitpicking. As long as she's got a job, Grace doesn't care if the guys call her a "throbbing mattress kitten." When a female co-worker objects to being called a girl, Grace grins:

> I'm thirty-five. I have three children. I can hide a can of cat food under each breast. If he thinks I'm a girl, I like it.

One of sitcom's most wrenching moments occurs when Grace's little boy reveals that he knows the family secret: Daddy beat up Mommy. The moment, played for real, not for laughs, pushes the envelope on what's allowable on a show that still winds up funny. (We've come a long way, baby, since *The Honeymooners* Ralph Kramden got laughs by balling up a fist and threatening to send Alice "to the moon!"

Pushed by independent performers and producers, situation comedy has expanded its willingness to reflect American lives. As talk-show trained audiences demand more realism (and scandal), sitcoms include more minority groups (ethnic, homosexual, disabled, etc.) and social issues. (Ever conscious of ratings, networks play catch-up at what feels like a snail's pace to those who are still excluded.) Still, as television searches for grist for its entertainment mill, it looks increasingly to reality to provide both soap opera/courtroom drama (O.J. Simpson) and comedy (autobiographical stand-up acts).

Still unlikely to make it to network TV is Reno, a peroxide-blond hurricane, who has been labeled "The Madonna of Comedy." Originally billed as a radical lesbian from San Francisco, she now omits homosexual or drug references—but that's the only thing that's been toned down. Hurling herself across the stage, she pantomimes an orgasm that climaxes in shrieks of ecstasy—then notes: "At this point, the person you have given your love to could be a radiator for all you care."

Reno also takes on the anti-abortion far-right:

Soon a cop will be at the door saying: "So I hear you had a miscarriage. Prove it."

And she casts a baleful eye on Yuppie feminists:

I burned my bra so this 24 year old broad could trade futures on Wall Street?

If Roseanne challenges the notion of fat as embarrassing, Reno challenges the idea that any part of the female body is shameful or a suitable subject for smirking coyness or obscene jokes. For her show's finale, she does a lyrical collage of the slang terms for female genitalia:

"Snatch." It's so Freudian, Like, I'm going to snatch that thing...."
Beaver—" I don't get it. Do you? I mean, I don't see any resemblance..."Poontang"—sounds like a breakfast drink.

Where Reno kids the language of sexist gynecology, the Clichettes, a three-woman comedy team, take visual pokes at the male anatomy. As James Brown's song "It's a Man's Man's Man's World" blasts over the sound system, the Clichettes lip-synch the lyrics, wielding electric guitars—and outfitted in nude drag. Exploring their muscular male "bodies" for new areas to stick their removable penises, the comediennes settle for the conventional place. Then, unzipping their torsos, they strip down to the parochial school dresses they are wearing underneath. Donning beehive wigs, they lip-synch the words to a 1950s pop ode to the transforming power of finding a boyfriend.

Equally outrageous is Judy Tenuta, self-styled "petite flower." Dressed in tattered chiffon and accessorized with an accordion, she tucks a blossom in her long, dark curls, curls her lip in contemptuous fury at male audience members, and spits out "stud puppets!" When Tenuta was starting her career, clients paid her to deliver "insult telegrams" to their spouses. Now she takes on all comers—including her own romantic fantasies. In a high, wispy voice, she reminisces: "When I was about to get married...." Then, suddenly possessed by her own *Exorcist-style* demon, she snarls at the disbelieving audience: "*Itcouldhappen!*"

Her taste in men?—"big, beefy burritos of manhood with the brains of handi-wipes." A spaced-out dominatrix, she dreams of an S&M relationship with Santa Claus. Then, settling for what's available, she invites a male audience member onstage and rides him bareback while lashing the air with a bullwhip.

Tenuta's persona plays with polarization—ultra-feminine costume elements and ultra-macho aggression. Other comediennes are more gender neutral. Ellen DeGeneres (star of the Disney-sponsored sitcom *Ellen)* an attractive, wholesome blonde, and Paula Poundstone, a rangy, casually elegant brunette, wear loose slacks and shirts and work with less sexually oriented material. DeGeneres says:

> I don't even consider myself a female comedienne. I'm a comedian. My gender doesn't come into it. I don't bring being a woman into my act. I just talk about people. A lot of guys like that. I don't separate them out.

DeGeneres' good-humored act is based on everday absurdities:

> Does this ever happen to you? People come up to you in the street and ask, "Do you have any loose change?" Like we normally carry it around in these bank rolls. "Sorry. Love to help you. But I can't crack it. It's in the roll."

Poundstone delivers much of her comedy plopped on a stool, befuddled by the oddness of existence. On a recent trip to Texas, she marvels at how she, an animal lover and the owner of two cats, could suddenly lust after leather boots.

> I developed this unnatural boot need. These boots are part lizard skin, part calf skin, so I hurt as many animals as I possibly could to get this footwear. I said, "Do you have anything in kittens?"

Today's women's comedy includes a wide range of physical types, styles, and material that ranges from the sexually neutral to a focus on women's areas: body image, feminine products, reproduction, and relationships. Jenny LeCoat, a British comedienne, does a routine about the pressures on an adolescent girl to be thin.

> I used to read *Jackie* (a magazine for teenage girls). This article advised, "Try to stand between the radiator and the wall. If you can't, you're a fat pig!"

Other comediennes do routines on the patronizing silliness of advertising for women, Viewing a television commercial for sanitary pads with "wings," Sandra Shamus dubs the product "The Pegasus of Pads!" She pantomimes dismounting from a bucking pad and being asked, "How d'ya get here?" Patting her invisible steed, she shrugs, "I took a pad."

Comedienne Angela Scott does a routine on childbirth.

> I gave birth in an amphitheater. More people were watching me than are here now. *Not* the position you want to be in when you're expecting company. My ex-husband was in the delivery room. They should have given him pom poms and a short skirt:
>
> "Push that baby! Push that baby !
>
> Out! Out! Out! Go girl! Go girl! Make that baby shout!"

Sometimes, comediennes mix women's issues with concerns about environment or racism. Shamus spoofs the idiocy of an ad for plastic tampon applicators that ignores women's intelligence, "I want my plastic!" Shaking her head at the stupidity of the ad, she comments:

> There's a hole in the ozone layer bigger than Antarctica. It takes two nuclear detonations to biodegrade plastic. Why would a woman want a trophy of her period well into the year 2000?

Racism rears its ugly—and funny—head in the context of women's romantic relationships. Black comedienne Kim Wayans does a routine about her experience with a Black nationalist boyfriend:

> I had this one boyfriend named Abdul. He was a Muslim. He made me feel so good about being black. He changed my name to Zula. Told me I was this beautiful African queen. He gave me incense to burn...He said, "Don't straighten your hair. Don't wear no make-up. Let your big lips shine." So he left me sittin' at home lookin' like Shaka Zulu; while he went out and got himself a white girl!

Comedienne Rhonda "Passion" Hansome jokes about yuppie fads and racial/religious persecution from the perspective of her own experience as an African-American woman.

> I predict that by the year 2000, calisthenics, aerobics and Nautilus will just be names that black folks call their children.

Her own interracial marriage to a white Jewish man has produced a son "whose nose doesn't know which way to grow," and who asks, "Mommy, have I been oppressed for 200 years or 2000?"

> I'm tired of the stereotype that all black families have unwed mothers, drug addicts and unemployment—all that's just in mine.

> I came from a very rough neighborhood, My mother was overprotective. She wouldn't let me play with certain kids in the neighborhood. They all said I thought I was white. I did not think I was white just because I was into photography, computers, and real estate. I thought I was Japanese.

Comedienne Geri Jewell gently tweaks her audience's discomfort with her own physical disability by announcing:

> I have cerebral palsy. Think of it as CP. But don't confuse it with MD MS VD AT&T or PMS...although I probably have that too.

Her identity as a woman and a disabled person mingle in jokes like:

> The worst thing about having CP is trying to pluck my eyebrows. How do you think I got pierced ears?

When Jewell wrote to her idol Carol Burnett, the older comedienne encouraged her to pursue her dream—a career in comedy. Jewell finally managed to attend a taping of *The Carol Burnett Show*, where she feigned deafness to get a front row seat. Carried away, she waved her hand for attention. When Burnett called on her, the usher explained that Jewell was deaf. "No I'm not!" she blurted out. As the audience stared, Jewell gulped, then cried out with religious fervor, "Oh my God! I can hear!"

Some critics have argued that female comics "ghettoize" themselves by overly focusing on "women's issues." If this is true, the reason may be that stand-up comedy has been overwhelming male-oriented, and the vast majority of stand-up comics are still men. Like any group whose experience is not the "norm" ie. racial/ethnic/religious minorities, the disabled, or homosexuals, women are conscious of the specialness of their experience.

Finally, it may simply not be true that women's comedy is more ghettoized than that of men. The perspective that is thought of as neutral is usually that of the dominant group, i.e., male. Stand-up comedy is a personal, often autobiographical art form, and comics relate to broad issues through personal experience. When white male comics do this, their perspective is taken as the norm. Emily Levine says:

> Men think their version of reality is the reality. And I'd like my version of reality to be the dominant one. When I walk on stage, I ask the audience to accept a different way of looking at things, and there's tension. I have to find a way to make my version of reality palatable to the audience,

Mo Gaffney, former host of HBO's comedy/talk show, *Women Aloud*, which provided a forum for women's issues and a showcase for comediennes, says:

> Comedy has always been what men thought was funny; now we have women's perspective. Couched in comedy, you can tell a lot of truth. Humor takes down defenses, so men don't automatically close themselves off. Today, there's less women's self-deprecating humor, and women can be both attractive and funny. The fact that there are more women comics puts a check on men's sexist humor. Now men have to work with women, go backstage and see a woman who is as powerful and funny as they are.

Michael Iopoce advises bonding with an audience by joking about subjects of common interest. "The locker room standbys are always a good bet: sports, business—or women." As women enter boardrooms and comedy clubs, speakers and performers will have to appeal to them, and the old locker room standbys will seem less "normal."

In fact, the signs of change are all around us. Lotus Weinstock says, "Ten years ago, a woman would not laugh before her date did, so if you did something from a woman's point of view, the woman wouldn't want to laugh and expose herself. Now, women will lead the crowd."

As more women enter the stand-up field, they challenge the notion of comedy as phallic aggression. Comic Paul Provenza describes a situation where someone in the audience grabbed his microphone as "like having your balls grabbed—you have no control," and several male comics use the analogy of the "microphone as dick" to justify why there are so few women in stand-up comedy.

But Robin Tyler says:

When male comics are talking about stand-up being phallic, what they're talking about is aggressively controlling an audience, and women aren't supposed to be allowed this. My answer to that is, 'Tough shit!' They think, somehow, the prick is the most aggressive thing, and that's not true; the mind is much more powerful than the prick—and the mind doesn't go down in two minutes.

Comedienne Jenny LeCoat says:

Stand up comedy is aggressive. Especially with some audiences. If you're not as aggressive as they know they're going to be, they'll smell that inability to cope a mile off, and they'll have you.

Then, reconsidering, she adds:

Aggression is the wrong word. Aggression comes from fear. It's the other side of fear. What you're talking about is confidence.

Just as there is no single model for women comics, there are many ways of relating to audiences—from aggressive domination to mystical union. Sandra Shamus says:

You have two circles. This is the audience, and this is the performer. When they mesh, that little space, it's the sweet spot. You're standing like a lightning rod for creativity and something shoots into you and out of your mouth, and the audience is screaming, and so are you. And you think, "How did I think of that?" And you didn't. It was divine intervention somehow. Robin Williams talks about being in the whole Zen of it, just opening his mouth and this torrent of gifts comes out.

Brett Butler says:

When comedy works, its is a circle that goes from the performer to the crowd and back again. Although the comedian is the one elevated on the stage and illuminated by light, the audience participates just as directly in the process. Like the moment in sex in which both partners "become as one," the room is filled with the uniting of spirits for a common cause.

Will stand-up comedy ever be a sexually neutral profession? Will stand-up comedy evolve toward a model of shared creative inspiration and away from a model of aggressive domination? Or is stand-up comedy, as many suggest, inherently aggressive? And does that mean that it will continue to attract mainly male performers? Will the problems of the stand-up life-style—the constant travel, the problems establishing a relationship, and the often crude, confrontive atmosphere in the clubs continue to discourage women from pursuing this career? Or will women simply deal with the stress as they have with the demands of other high-stress professions; and will their proportion increase until they are on par with men?

The sheer numbers of stand-up comics and sketch artists are few, but their importance extends beyond statistics and small venues. Whether it's the next Roseanne, Brett Butler, Phyllis Diller, or Joan Rivers playing a tiny comedy club, or the next Whoopi Goldberg or Lily Tomlin touring a one-woman show, or the next Carol Burnett or Lucille Ball trying out a sketch act, it is out of these artistic trenches that the new feminine sensibility will emerge.

More and more woman are finding comedy a vehicle to express their feelings, ideas, and lives. As female performers, writers, directors and producers become more prominent and powerful, their humor is evolving away from the self-deprecating comedy of appeasement and toward the confrontive comedy of personal truth.

As comediennes dispute old, sexist ideas about what is funny or real, everyone is challenged. Both male and female comics are challenged to be more honest and original. Audiences are challenged to listen to new, sometimes radical ideas—and laugh at the stupidity of accepted ways of thinking. A laugh is a vote of understanding that no one can deny. In that vote is, eventually, a revolution.

Notes (by order of appearance of subject)

"You Can't Deep Freeze a Red-Hot Mama" as quoted in Sarah Blacher Cohen, "The Unkosher Comediennes," *Jewish Wry*, (Bloomington: Indiana University Press, 1987) p.107.

Sophie Tucker, *Some of These Days*, (New York: Doubleday, 1945).

Belle Barth, as quoted in Sarah Blacher Cohen, "The Unkosher Comediennes," *Jewish Wry*, p.113.

Jackie"Moms" Mabley, as quoted in Linda Martin and Kerry Segrave, *Women in Comedy* (Secaucus, New Jersey, Citadel Press, 1986), p.289.

Lily Tomlin as quoted in Linda Martin and Kerry Segrave, *Women in Comedy*, p.371.

Lee Israel, "Lily Tomlin: Good-bye to Duddiness," *Ms*. p.88.

Louise Bernikow, "Excuse Me? Do you know who Lily Tomlin Is?" *Playgirl*, July 1976.

Lily Tomlin, personal interview, conducted at the Hyatt Regency Reunion Towers, Dallas,Texas 1980.

Diane Judge "Talking with Lily Tomlin," *Redbook Magazine*, p.16.

Richard Corliss, "Bette Steals Hollywood," *Time*, March 2, 1987, p.66.

Bette Midler, as quoted in Roz Warren (editor), *Revolutionary Laughter*, (Freedom, CA: The Crossing Press,1995) p.156.

Susan Dworkin, "The Making of *The Color Purple*." *Ms*. December, 1985.

Jill Kearny, "Whoopi Goldberg: Color Her Anything," *American Film*, December, 1985.

Totie Fields, as quoted in Al Cohn "Gets Fat on Laughs," *Newsday*, December 17, 1966, p.13W

Playgirl, January, 1975, p.82.

Phyllis Diller, personal interview.

Joan Levine, "The Feminine Routine," *Journal of Communication*, 26 (3): Summer, 1976.

Samuel Janus, "The Psychology of Comedy," *American Journal of Psychoanalysis*. June, 1978.

Joy Behar, personal interview conducted by telephone, 1993.

Lotus Weinstock, personal interview conducted in her home in Los Angeles, CA, August, 1981.

D.C. Dennison, "Paula Poundstone," *The Boston Globe*, September 27, 1987.

Susan Horowitz, "Queen of Comedy: Sandra Bernhard" *New York Talk*, May 8, 1988.

Phil Berger, "The New Comediennes," *The New York Times Magazine*, July 29, 1984.

Adrienne Tolsch, personal interview conducted at her home in New York, NY, 1987.

Emily Yoffe, "The Darling of Deadpan: Rita Rudner," *Lear's* .

Hank Gallo, "Rita Rudner Makes HBO's 'Night' a Real Laugher," *Daily News*.

Kevin Sessums, "Roseanne," *Vanity Fair*, February 2, 1994.

Joy Horowitz, "June Cleaver Without Pearls," *The New York Times*, October 16, 1988.

Mary Murphy, "Brett Under Fire," *TV Guide*, June 17, 1995.

Harry Waters, "Three Stars Are Born: The Wrath of Grace," *Newsweek*, October 25, 1993.

Stephen Fenichell, "Funny Ladies," *Philip Morris Magazine*, March-April, 1990.

Rhonda "Passion" Hansome, personal interview conducted at her home in New York, NY, 1993.

Geri Jewell, personal interview conducted by telephone, 1993.

Mo Gaffney, personal interview conducted in New York, NY 1993.

General Sources

Betsy Born, *Comic Lives:Inside the World of American Stand-Up Comedy*, (New York: Simon & Schuster, 1987)

Samuel Harris, "Comedienne Reveal How to Keep a Sense of Humor," *The Advertiser*, Wednesday, March 5, 1986.

Stephen Holden, "Comedy Bad Boys Screech Into the Spotlight," *The New York Times*, February 28, 1988,

Joyce Purnick, "The Legacy of Mary Richards," *The New York Times*, February 2, 1991.

Recordings of Live Performances and Television Programs

Whoopi Goldberg on Broadway, New York, 1984.

Grace Under Fire, ABC.

Roseanne, ABC.

Ellen, ABC.

Reno, *Reno in Rage and Rehab,* comedy/perfomance piece.

Lily Tomlin, *The Search for Signs of Intelligent Life in the Universe,* written with Jane Wagner, February 3, 1986.

Wisecracks: a documentary film directed by Gail Singer, Alliance International, The National Film Board of Canada, May 27,1992, 23 Prince Andrew Place, Toronto, Canada M3C 2H2. (Publicity: Lauren Hyman, 799 Greenwich St., New York, NY 10014.

Sources

Behar, Joy, personal interview conducted by telephone, 1993.

Bernikow, Louise, "Excuse Me? Do you know who Lily Tomlin Is?" *Playgirl,* July 1976.

Berger, Phil, "The New Comediennes," *The New York Times Magazine,* July 29, 1984.

Blacher-Cohen, Sarah "The Unkosher Comediennes," *Jewish Wry,* (Bloomington: Indiana University Press, 1987) pp.107, 113, 4

Born, Betsy, *Comic Lives: Inside the World of American Stand-Up Comedy,* (New York: Simon & Schuster, 1987)

Cohn, Al "Gets Fat on Laughs," *Newsday,* December 17, 1966, p.13W

Corliss, Richard, "Bette Steals Hollywood," *Time,* March 2, 1987, p.66.

Dennison, D.C., "Paula Poundstone," *The Boston Globe,* September 27, 1987.

Diller, Phyllis, personal interview conducted at her hotel suite at the Tropican Hotel in Atlantic City, New Jersey, November 7, 1984.

Dworkin, Susan, "The Making of *The Color Purple.*" Ms. December 1985.

Ellen, ABC Television.

Fenichell, Stephen, "Funny Ladies," *Philip Morris Magazine,* March-April, 1990.

Gallo, Hank, "Rita Rudner Makes HBO's 'Night' a Real Laugher," *Daily News,*

Gaffney, Mo, personal interview conducted in New York, NY 1993.

Grace Under Fire, (Premiere), ABC Television 1993.

Harris, Samuel, "Comedienne Reveal How to Keep a Sense of Humor," *The Advertiser,* Wednesday, March 5, 1986.

Hansome, Rhonda "Passion," personal interview conducted at her home in New York, NY, 1993.

Holden, Stephen, "Comedy Bad Boys Screech Into the Spotlight," *The New York Times,* February 28, 1988,

Horowitz, Joy, "June Cleaver Without Pearls," *The New York Times,* October 16, 1988.

Israel, Lee, "Lily Tomlin: Good-bye to Duddiness," *Ms.* p.88.

Janus, Samuel, "The Psychology of Comedy," *American Journal of Psychoanalysis.* June 1978.

Judge, Diane "Talking with Lily Tomlin," *Redbook Magazine,* p.16.

Kearny, Jill, "Whoopi Goldberg: Color Her Anything," *American Film,* December, 1985.

Levine, Joan, "The Feminine Routine," *Journal of Communication,* 26 (3): Summer, 1976.

Martin, Linda and Segrave, Kerry, *Women in Comedy* (Secaucus, New Jersey, Citadel Press, 1986), p.289, 290, 371.

Murphy, Mary, "Brett Under Fire," *TV Guide,* June 17, 1995.

Playgirl, January, 1975, p.82.

Tucker, Sophie, *Some of These Days,* (New York: Doubleday, 1945).

Purnick, Joyce, "The Legacy of Mary Richards," *The New York Times,* February 2, 1991.

Reno in Rage and Rehab, comedy/perfomance piece

L

Roseanne, ABC Television.

Sessums, Kevin, "Roseanne," *Vanity Fair,* February 2, 1994.

Tolsch, Adrienne, personal interview conducted at her home in New York, NY, 1987.

Tomlin, Lily, personal interview, conducted at the Hyatt Regency Reunion Towers, Dallas,Texas 1980.

Tomlin, Lily, *The Search for Signs of Intelligent Life in the Universe,* written with Jane Wagner, February 3, 1986.

Warren, Roz Editor, *Revolutionary Laughter,* (Freedom, CA: The Crossing Press,1995) p.156.

Waters, Harry, "Three Stars Are Born: The Wrath of Grace," *Newsweek,* October 25, 1993.

Weinstock, Lotus, personal interview conducted in her home in Los Angeles, California, August, 1981.

Whoopi Goldberg on Broadway, New York, 1984.

Wisecracks: a documentary film directed by Gail Singer, Produced by Gail Singer and Signe Johansson in co-production with Zinger Films and The National Film Board of Canada, Distributed by Alliance International, 23 Prince Andrew Place, Toronto, Canada M3C 2H2. © 1991,(Publicity: Lauren Hyman, 799 Greenwich St., New York, NY 10014).

Bibliography

Books and Periodicals

Allen, Steve, with Wollman, Jane. *How To Be Funny: Discovering the Comic In You.* New York: McGraw-Hill Book Company, 1987.

Andrews, Bart. *Lucy & Ricky & Fred & and Ethel: The Story of "I Love Lucy."* New York: Fawcett Popular Library, 1976.

Andrews, Bart and Thomas Watson. *Loving Lucy.* New York: St. Martin's Press, 1980.

Ansen, David with Janet Huck. "The Great Goldie Rush." *Newsweek.* January 12, 1981.

Aristotle. The Poetic. Chapter V. as quoted in Clark Barret H. Revised by Henry Popkin. *European Theories of the Drama.* New York: Crown Publishers Inc. 1965.

Arnaz, Desi. *A Book.* New York: Warner Books, 1976.

Ball, Lucille. Transcription of seminar sponsored by the *American Film Institute.* Los Angeles, California, 1972.

Barreca, Regina. *Last Laughs: Perspectives on Women in Comedy.* New York, London, Paris: Gordon and Breach 1988.

Barreca, Regina. *They Used to Call Me Snow White...But I Drifted: Women's Strategic Use of Humor.* New York: Viking Publishers 1991.

Bego, Mark. *Bette Midler Outrageously Divine.* A Signet Book. New American Library. New York: 1987.

Bergson, Henri. "Laughter" 1900. Fred Rothwell, tr. in *Comedy.* Willie Sypher, ed. New York: Doubleday & Company, 1956.

Borns, Betsy. *Comic Lives.* A Fireside Book published by Simon and Schuster, Inc. New York: 1987.

Burnett, Carol. *One More Time.* New York: Random House, 1986.

Burrows, Abe. *Cactus Flower.* based on a play by Pierre Barillet and Jean Pierre Credy. New York: Samuel French, Inc. 1966.

Carter, Judy. *Stand-Up Comedy: The Book* A Dell Trade Paperback.Bantam, Doubleday Dell Publishing Group, Inc. New York: 1989.

Chapman, Anthony J. and Hugh C. Foot. *Humor and Laughter: Theory, Research, and Applications.* New York: John Wiley and Sons 1979.

Clark, Barrett H. Revised by Henry Popkin. *European Theories of the Drama.* New York: Crown Publishers, Inc. 1965

Cohen, Al."[Totie Fields]...Gets Fat on Laughs." *Newsday.* December 17, 1966.

Cohen, Sarah Blacher ed., *From Hester Street to Hollywood: The Jewish American Stage and Screen.* Bloomington: Indiana University Press, 1983.

Cohen, Sarah Blacher. *Jewish Wry.* Bloomington and Indianapolis: Indiana University Press, 1987.

Collier, Denise and Kathleen Beckett. *Spare Ribs: Women in the Humor Biz.* New York: St. Martin's Press, 1980.

Coquelin, Constant. "Have Women a Sense of Humor?" *Harper's Bazaar.* 36:497-98. July, 1902.

Davis,Jacalyn. "Hansome Is As Hansome Does." *The Friar's Epistle.* March, 1991

Denison, D.C. "The Interview: Paula Poundstone." *The Boston Globe Magazine.* September 27, 1987.

Diller, Phyllis. *The Joys of Aging and How To Avoid Them.* Garden City, New York. Doubleday & Company 1981.

Dworkin, Susan. "Carol Burnett—Getting On With It." *Ms.* September, 1983.

Dutka, Elaine. "Slightly To the Left of Normal." *Time.* May 8, 1989.

Dworkin, Susan. "Roseanne Barr: The Disgruntled Housewife as a Stand-Up Comedienne." *Ms.* October, 1984.

Edmond, Georgina. "Is There Anything Joan Rivers Won't Talk About?" *Spotlight.* June, 1992.

Eftimados, Maria. "Local Laughs" *The West Side Spirit.* June 4, 1989.

Engel, Jane. "Comedians' Lament:'Take My Hangups.'" *The Tribune.* January 14, 1976.

Ervilino, Bill. "A Hot and Sassy Mix." *The New York Post.* January 17, 1990

Fischer, Seymore and Rhoda. *Pretend the World is Funny and Forever.* New York: Random House, 1981.

Freud, Sigmund. *Jokes and Their Relation to the Unconscious.* Newly Translated from the German and edited by James Stachey. New York, London: W.W. Norton & Company, 1963.

Gallo, Hank. "Rita Rudner Makes HBO's 'Night' a Real Laugher." *Daily News.*

Goldsmith, Oliver. "An Essay on the Theatre: Or, A Comparison between Laughing and Sentimental Comedy." As quoted in Clark, Barrett H. Revised by Henry Popkin. *European Theories of the Drama.* New York: Crown Publishers, Inc. 1965.

Harris, Samela. "Comediennes Reveal How to Keep a Sense of Humor." *The Advertiser.* March 5, 1986.

Hawn, Goldie. Interview Printed in *Playboy.* January, 1985.

Hellitzer, Melvin. *Comedy Writing Secrets.* Writers Digest Books. Cincinnati, Ohio: 1987.

Hirshberg, Lynn. "I Love Lucy." *Rolling Stone.* June, 1983.

Holden, Stephen."Comedy's Bad Boys Screech Into the Spotlight" *The New York Times.* February 28, 1988.

Holmes, John. "Female Comics: Coming On Strong and Funny." *The Washington Times Magazine.* November 26, 1992.

Hopkins,Ellen. "Who's Laughing Now? Women." *The New York Times.* September 16, 1990.

Horowitz, Susan. "Sitcom Domesticus: A Species Endangered by Social Change." *Channels of Communication. Anthologized in Television: The Critical View,* Edited by Horace Newcomb. Oxford University Press. New York, Oxford 1987.

Horowitz, Susan. "Life With Kate and Allie." *Ms.* September, 1984.

Horowitz, Susan. "Carol Burnett Gets a Kick Out of Annie." *American Film.* May, 1982.

Horowitz, Susan. "Women Comics Come On Strong." *Los Angeles Herald Examiner.* September 1, 1981.

Horowitz, Susan. "Where the Laughs Are: New York's Comedy Clubs." *Good Housekeeping.* November, 1979.

Iapoce, Michael. *A Funny Thing Happened on the Way to the Boardroom: Using Humor in Public Speaking.* New York: John Wiley & Sons, Inc. 1988.

Irwin, Rhoda. "Goldie." *Rolling Stone.* March 5, 1981.

Janus, Samuel. "The Comic Personality." *The American Journal of Psychoanalysis.* January, 1981.

Janus, Samuel. "The Psychology of Comedy." *The American Journal of Psychoanalysis.* June, 1978.

Janus, Samuel. "Humor, Sex, and Power in American Society." *The American Journal of Psychoanalysis.* Summer, 1981.

Jonson, Ben. "Dedication to Volpone." as quoted in Clark, Barrett H. Revised by Henry Popkin. *European Theories of the Drama.* New York: Crown Publishers Inc. 1965.

Judge, Diane. "Talking With Lily Tomlin." *Redbook Magazine.* January, 1981.

Kazan, Nick. "Lily Tomlin Takes Her Chances." *Village Voice.* 20: 88. February 24, 1975.

Kerr, Peter. "Situation Comedies Come to Grief." *The New York Times.* April 1, 1984

Klein, Julia. "The New Stand-Up Comics." *Ms.* October, 1984.

Lardine, Bob. "Totie Fields: A Heavy Favorite." *New York Sunday News.* February, 1967.

Lauter, Paul, gen. ed. *Theories of Comedy.* Plato. Philebus. New York: Anchor Books, Doubleday & Company, 1964.

Levine, Joan. "The Feminine Routine." *Journal of Communication.* 26:(3): Summer, 1976.

Martin, Linda and Kerry Segrave. *Women in Comedy.* Secaucus, New Jersey: Citadel Press, 1986.

Mast, Gerald. *The Comic Mind: Comedy and the Movies.* Indianapolis/ New York: Bobbs Merrill, 1973.

McCrohan, Donna. *The Second City: A Backstage History of Comedy's Hottest Troupe.* A Perigree Book. New York: Putnam Publishing Group 1987.

McGee, Paul. "Humor: Its Origin and Development," *Psychology Today.* May, 1981.

Mellencamp, Patrica. *High Anxiety: Catastrophe, Scandal, Age, & Comedy.* Bloomington and Indianapolis: Indiana University Press, 1992.

Meryman, Richard. "Carol Burnett's Own Story." *McCall's.* February, 1976.

Mindess, Harvey. "Study of the Comic Personality." *The American Journal of Psychoanalysis.* October, 1973.

Moliere, Jean Baptiste Poquelin. "Preface to Tartuffe." as quoted in Clark Barret H. Revised by Henry Popkin. *European Theories of the Drama.* New York: Crown Publishers Inc. 1965.

Parish, James Robert. Printed Transcript of a Personal Interview with Phyllis Diller conducted at the *American Film Institute.* October, 1977.

Quindlen, Anna. "Catch a Rising Comic: Four Comics." *The New York Times.* December 8, 1978.

Rivers, Joan. with Richard Meryman. *Enter Talking.* New York: Delacorte Press, 1986.

Rivers, Joan. with Richard Meryman. *Still Talking.* New York: Turtle Bay Books/Random House, 1991.

Rosen, Marjorie. *Popcorn Venus: Women, Movies, and the American Dream.* New York: Avon Books, 1973

Royalty, Doug. "An Entertainment Harlot: Adrienne Tolsch." *The Champaign Urbana News Gazette.* October 5, 1984.

Schindler, Arlene. "When Tolsch Goes Solo, She Sparkles and Shines." *New York Post.* December 24, 1992.

Stevenson, Ray. "Inside Phyllis Diller." *Redbook,* August, 1978.

Tauber, Peter. "Jay Leno: Not Just a Funny Face." *The New York Times Magazine.* February 26, 1989.

Totie Fields. "Playgirl Interview." *Playgirl.* January, 1975.

Tucker, Ernest."Rhonda Hansome Carves Out Career" *Chicago Sun Times.* August 18, 1989.

Tucker, Sophie. *Some of These Days.* New York: Doubleday 1945

Walker, Nancy A. *A Very Serious Thing: Women's Humor and American Culture.* Minneapolis: University of Minnesota Press 1988.

Warren, Roz. *Revolutionary Laughter: The World of Women Comics.* Freedom, California: The Crossing Press, 1995.

Weinstock, Lotus. *The Lotus Position.* Toronto, New York, London, Sydney: Bantam Books, 1982.

Walton, Mary."Borderline Funny." *The Philadelphia Inquirer Magazine.* February 11, 1990.

Witty, Susan. "The Laugh Makers." *Psychology Today.* August, 1983.

Zolotow, Maurice. "The Two Lives of Phyllis Diller." *50 Plus.* July, 1979.

Plays, Films, Television Shows, Nightclub Acts, Etc.

Burnett, Carol. Interview with Barbara Walters. NBC. May 12, 1983.

Diller, Phyllis. Nightclub Act performed at the Tropicana Hotel. November, 1984.

The Carol Burnett Show. CBS: 1966–1977.

The Gary Moore Show. CBS. June 12, 1957.

I Love Lucy. CBS Television. 1951–1960.

Jewell, Geri. Maya Association, Videotaped at Raggs, New York, New York. August 1, 1989.

Julie and Carol at Carnegie Hall. CBS: June 11, 1962.

Once Upon a Mattress. CBS Television. December 12, 1972

Private Benjamin. Warner Brothers. 1980. Written by Charles Snyder, Harvey Miller, and Nancy Meyers, and directed by Howard Zieff.

Rivers, Joan. *The Next to Last Joan Rivers Album.* (phonograph recording). Arista Records BLS-8096. New York.

Rivers, Joan. *What Becomes a Semi-Legend Most* (phonograph recording). Geffen Records Los Angeles, California.

Rowan and Martin's Laugh-In. NBC: January, 1968 to May, 1973.

The Search for Signs of Intelligent Life in the Universe. Starring and Produced by Lily Tomlin. Written and Directed by Jane Wagner. New York: Plymouth Theatre 1986.

Tomlin, Lily. *Modern Scream.* (phonograph recording). Polydor PD 6051. New York, 1975.

Tomlin, Lily. *This Is a Recording.* (phonograph recording). Polydor stereo 24-4055 New York, 1971.

Tucker, Sophie. *Sophie Tucker's Greatest Hits.*(phonograph recording). Cameo. CBS 32318. collection made 1983.

Wisecracks. (documentary film). Directed by Gail Singer, Produced by Gail Singer and Signe Johansson in co-production with Zinger Films and the National Film Board of Canada. Distributed by Alliance International, Toronto, Canada ©1991.

Women Aloud. (television program). produced by HBO Downtown Productions for Comedy Central. Unitel Studios, New York, NY: June, July, 1992.

Personal Interviews

Ball, Lucille. Personal Interview held at her home in New York, New York. April 14, 1984.

Behar, Joy. Personal Telephone Interviews held in New York, New York. September, 1992.

Bernhard, Sandra. Personal Telephone Interview held in New York, New York. November 9, 1983.

Burnett, Carol. Personal Interview held at the Polo Lounge in Los Angeles, California, June 22, 1982.

Clair, Dick. Personal Interview held at the home of Jenna McMahon. Hollywood, California. June 22, 1982.

Diller, Phyllis. Personal Interview held at the Tropicana Hotel in Atlantic City, New Jersey. November 7, 1984.

Gaffney, Mo. Personal Interview held in her dressing room at the HBO studio after the taping of *Women Aloud.* July, 1992.

Hansome, Rhonda "Passion" Personal Interview held at her home in New York, New York: October, 1991

McMahon, Jenna. Personal Interview held at her home in Hollywood, California: June 22, 1982.

Poltrack, David. Vice-President of CBS Television. Personal Interview conducted in his office on May 19, 1985.

Rivers, Joan. Personal Interview held at her home in Bel Aire, California. October, 1979.

Tolsch, Adrienne.Personal Interview held at her home in New York, New York: November, 1987.

Tomlin, Lily. Personal Interview held at the Anatole Hotel in Dallas Texas, 1980.

Sobieski, Carol. Personal Interview held on the set of the film *Annie.* Los Angeles, California: June 9, 1982.

Weinstock, Lotus. Personal Interview held in her home in Los Angeles, California: June, 1981